Company's Coming®

Breakfasts
On the Go

Jean Paré

www.companyscoming.com
visit our website

Front Cover:
Out-the-door Rolls, page 10

Back Cover:
Top Left: Mexican Egg Wraps, page 20
Top Right: Paradise Smoothie, page 72
Bottom Left: Egg and Pepper Burritos, page 86
Bottom Right: Make-ahead Benedict, page 114

Front Flap:
Egg and Cheese Burgers, page 12
Apricot Breakfast Drink, page 64
Morning Burritos, page 84
Buckwheat Sunrise, page 124
Apple Raisin French Toast, page 142

Back Flap:
Spiced Sweet Potato Muffins, page 42

Breakfasts on the Go

Copyright © Company's Coming Publishing Limited

First Printing July 2013
Library and Archives Canada Cataloguing in Publication
Paré, Jean, date
Breakfasts on the go / Jean Paré.
(Original series)
Includes index.
At head of title: Company's Coming.
ISBN 978-1-927126-53-0
1. Breakfasts. 2. Cookbooks. I. Title. II. Series: Paré,
Jean, date. Original series.
TX733.P373 2013   641.5'2   C2013-900350-9

Published by
Company's Coming Publishing Limited
2311 – 96 Street
Edmonton, Alberta, Canada T6N 1G3
Tel: 780-450-6223   Fax: 780-450-1857
www.companyscoming.com

Company's Coming is a registered trademark owned by
Company's Coming Publishing Limited

We acknowledge the financial support of the Government
of Canada through the Canada Book Fund for our
publishing activities.

Printed in China

PC: 16

TABLE OF CONTENTS

THE COMPANY'S COMING STORY

Jean Paré (pronounced "jeen PAIR-ee") grew up understanding that the combination of family, friends and home cooking is the best recipe for a good life. From her mother, she learned to appreciate good cooking, while her father praised even her earliest attempts in the kitchen. When Jean left home, she took with her a love of cooking, many family recipes and an intriguing desire to read cookbooks as if they were novels!

> "*Never share a recipe you wouldn't use yourself.*"

When her four children had all reached school age, Jean volunteered to cater the 50th anniversary celebration of the Vermilion School of Agriculture, now Lakeland College, in Alberta, Canada. Working out of her home, Jean prepared a dinner for more than 1,000 people, launching a flourishing catering operation that continued for over 18 years. During that time, she had countless opportunities to test new ideas with immediate feedback—resulting in empty plates and contented customers! Whether preparing cocktail sandwiches for a house party or serving a hot meal for 1,500 people, Jean Paré earned a reputation for great food, courteous service and reasonable prices.

As requests for her recipes increased, Jean was often asked the question, "Why don't you write a cookbook?" Jean responded by teaming up with her son, Grant Lovig, in the fall of 1980 to form Company's Coming Publishing Limited. The publication of *150 Delicious Squares* on April 14, 1981 marked the debut of what would soon become one of the world's most popular cookbook series.

The company has grown since those early days when Jean worked from a spare bedroom in her home. Nowadays every Company's Coming recipe is *kitchen-tested* before it is approved for publication.

Company's Coming cookbooks are distributed in Canada, the United States, Australia and other world markets. Bestsellers many times over in English, Company's Coming cookbooks have also been published in French and Spanish.

Familiar and trusted in home kitchens around the world, Company's Coming cookbooks are offered in a variety of formats. Highly regarded as kitchen workbooks, the softcover Original Series, with its lay-flat plastic comb binding, is still a favourite among readers.

Jean Paré's approach to cooking has always called for *quick and easy recipes* using *everyday ingredients*. That view has served her well. The recipient of many awards, including the Queen Elizabeth Golden Jubilee Medal, Jean was appointed Member of the Order of Canada, her country's highest lifetime achievement honour.

Jean continues to share what she calls The Golden Rule of Cooking: *Never share a recipe you wouldn't use yourself.* It's an approach that has worked—*millions of times over!*

FOREWORD

They say breakfast is the most important meal of the day, but for many of us, it also the most rushed, the most hectic, and unfortunately, the most-often skipped.

Hurrying out the door to get the kids to school or to get to work can mean that you don't have time to enjoy a good, nutritious meal. At best, you might reach for the packaged cereals, many of which have dubious nutritional value and are loaded with sugar, or slap some bread in the toaster. How enticing is that? Your taste buds are most likely bored enough to lead you back to bed and tuck you in. Why get up for humdrum food?

To have a good day, you need to start it off right, and that means filling your empty belly with wholesome food that will keep you happy and satisfied all morning long.

At Company's Coming, we know how crazy mornings can be, so we've created *Breakfast on the Go,* a collection of 75 tasty, nutritious recipes for people on the move.

Got an early morning meeting? Grab a Bacon Herb Muffin or slice of Banana Avocado Bread to eat on the way. Not much of an appetite in the morning?

Try a Berry Bran Shake for a light but healthy breakfast in a glass. Thinking about hitting the drive-thru for a breakfast sandwich? Throw together a Mexican Egg Wrap instead. Your wallet and your palate will thank you!

Breakfasts on the Go puts the "fast" in breakfast without sacrificing quality or taste. We've also included recipes you can prepare beforehand so they are ready in less time in the morning, as well as quick recipes for days like weekends that are not as rushed, when you have a few more minutes before racing out the door.

Whatever your day looks like, there are recipes in this cookbook that will suit your breakfast needs!

Jean Paré

Nutrition Information Guidelines

Each recipe is analyzed using the most current versions of the Canadian Nutrient File from Health Canada, and the United States Department of Agriculture (USDA) Nutrient Database for Standard Reference.

- If more than one ingredient is listed (such as "butter or hard margarine"), or if a range is given (1 – 2 tsp., 5 – 10 mL), only the first ingredient or first amount is analyzed.
- Milk used is 1% M.F. (milk fat), unless otherwise stated.
- Cooking oil used is canola oil, unless otherwise stated.
- Ingredients indicating "sprinkle," "optional" or "for garnish" are not included in the nutrition information.
- The fat in recipes and combination foods can vary greatly depending upon the sources and types of fats used in each specific ingredient. For these reasons, the amount of saturated, monounsaturated and polyunsaturated fats may not add up to the total fat content.

THE CASE FOR BREAKFAST

In today's busy world, who couldn't use a little extra sleep? A few pushes of the snooze button might seem like a good idea at the time, but you'll regret sacrificing breakfast for sleep when your stomach is rumbling part way through the morning. After six to eight hours of sleep, the body is ready for some fuel; you don't expect your car to drive for hours with no gas, and you shouldn't expect your body to keep going strong either without healthy foods to fuel it.

Studies have shown that kids who eat breakfast outperform those who do not— they are more productive and more focused, and they get better grades in school. Much the same can be said for adults in the workplace—a well-nourished body translates to a more effective worker. It's difficult to focus on the task at hand when you are overwhelmed with hunger pains.

Some people choose to skip breakfast in a misguided attempt to lose or maintain their weight, but in truth missing the morning meal usually has the opposite affect. Studies show that those who routinely skip breakfast actually tend to *gain* weight because they overeat at the next meal and make poor food choices, opting for high-calorie foods throughout the day.

Not only will your health benefit from eating a healthy breakfast, but so too will your pocketbook. You will be less tempted to swing through the drive-thru or grab something from the vending machine if you've already eaten a tasty, satisfying breakfast.

Although any food is better than no food, there are some obvious winners when it comes to breakfast fare, as far as what your body needs in the morning. Complex carbohydrates, fibre and protein will keep you going for hours; foods high in sugar will give you a short burst of energy that quickly fades, and so are not such good choices.

Apricot Breakfast Drink, page 64

THINKING AHEAD

Healthy breakfasts are not unachievable, even for the busiest among us; all it takes is a little planning.

If your mornings are too rushed for a sit down meal, choose portable items that you can eat on the go. Trying to eat a plate of scrambled eggs as you are navigating the morning commute is not a great idea, but snacking on a muffin, wrap or smoothie will fill you up and allow you to concentrate on the road. Or pack a breakfast that you can enjoy once you're at work, perhaps a bowl of oatmeal or a breakfast sandwich. Toss a breakfast cookie and some fruit into the kids' school bag to start their day off right.

If you have a little more time in the morning, you can opt for foods that can be prepared relatively quickly. Make-ahead meals are a great option because you do most of the work the night before, so the food makes it to the table in less time in the morning. For example, you could put together a make-ahead casserole as you are preparing dinner or when you have a little spare time in the evening. Slap it in the oven as soon as you get up the next morning, and by the time you finish your shower, a warm, comforting breakfast is ready and waiting.

Healthy Banana Cookies, page 54

THE FREEZER IS YOUR FRIEND

Although there are plenty of convenient breakfast foods available from grocery stores or fast food establishments, nothing beats homemade. Commercially made muffins and sweet breads can be expensive, are often high in fat and sugar and may contain preservatives—not really the best choice for your budget or your waistline. The same can be said for other packaged foods such as breakfast sandwiches, wraps and frozen waffles or pancakes. The good news is that you can prepare healthier, tastier versions of all these products (and more!) yourself and freeze them to have on hand when you need them. Again, all it takes is a little planning.

If you have time to whip up a batch of pancakes, great, why not double the batch and freeze the rest? You'll have pancakes accessible for busy weekday mornings that you can take out of the freezer and pop in the toaster for a quick, healthy, homemade breakfast. You can do the same with muffins, waffles, breakfast cookies, loaves, breakfast wraps, rolls, burritos... really, the possibilities are endless.

Guide to Freezing

To freeze pancakes, place them in a single layer on a baking sheet or wire rack until firm before transferring them to a plastic bag. Otherwise they will freeze into solid mass, and you'll have to thaw the whole batch at one time rather than grabbing one or two as you need them. You can also separate pancakes with waxed or parchment paper, if you prefer.

Wrap muffins and loaves in foil, then place them in a plastic bag; they'll be good in the freezer for about three months. If you can remember to take the items out of the freezer and thaw them overnight, all the better, but if you don't remember it's no big deal—they'll thaw in your bag on the way to work or school.

Many egg products do not freeze well, so we don't recommend freezing frittatas or the like. Wraps or burritos containing eggs are freezable, but the texture of the eggs may change, becoming rubbery. Your best bet would be to store such items in the fridge.

With anything that you are freezing, be sure to remove as much air as possible from the package before sealing it. Dry freezer air will rob your food of its moisture, leading to "freezer burned" items that, although not spoiled, are not nearly as tasty.

Spiced Sweet Potato Hash, page 92

THE RECIPES

The recipes in this book have been developed to provide healthy breakfast options with today's fast-paced lifestyle in mind. To fit into your busy day, breakfast fare must be quick to prepare, make-ahead or portable, and the recipes in this book are organized to reflect that reality.

On the Run:

The recipes in this section are portable, so you can eat them on the go. Most are prepared so you can grab them on the way out the door, but a few taste best when made fresh and don't take much time to complete.

Liquid Breakfasts:

As the name suggests, this section contains recipes for drinkable breakfasts, i.e., smoothies. Smoothies make fantastic breakfast fare. They are quick, easy, portable and versatile, and even kids love them. Most people think of fruit when they picture a smoothie, but you can sneak veggies, grains, tofu, nuts and many other nutritious foods into the blender, and the kids will be none the wiser. What a great way to take in a few of the recommended five to eight servings of fruit and veggies each day!

Sit Down Meals:

This section is made up of recipes for days that are not as rushed, when you have a little more time to sit with your family and enjoy a quick breakfast before heading out the door. The dishes can be prepared in less than 30 minutes.

Make-ahead Meals:

The make-ahead chapter of the book has recipe options in which most of the prep work is done in advance, so the food can make it to the table in a timely manner in the morning.

Weekend Fare:

Whether you have a day full of dropping kids at swimming lessons, rushing around doing errands or burning off some stress as a weekend warrior, you'll still need plenty of energy to make it through to your next meal. The recipes in this section take a bit longer to prepare, reflecting the slightly slower pace a weekend often allows, and the dishes are substantial enough to keep you going all morning long.

Frittata Muffins, page 32

Out-the-door Rolls

These rolls taste best warm, but they are also scrumptious cold. The dough must be chilled for at least 30 minutes before cooking, so to save time in the morning, prepare it the evening before and leave it in the fridge overnight. You can also prepare the dish in its entirety in advance if your mornings are particularly rushed; just grab it out of the fridge before you head out the door. The rolls will keep for up to five days in the fridge and up to three months in the freezer.

All-purpose flour	2 1/4 cups	300 mL
Granulated sugar	1 tbsp.	15 mL
Baking powder	2 tsp.	10 mL
Salt	1/2 tsp.	2 mL
Cooking oil	1/4 cup	60 mL
Milk	3/4 cup	175 mL
Lean ground pork	1 lb.	454 g
Lemon juice, fresh or bottled	1 1/2 tbsp.	25 mL
Green pepper, diced	1/2 cup	125 mL
Red pepper, diced	1/2 cup	125 mL
Chili powder	2 tsp.	10 mL
Dried oregano	3/4 tsp.	4 mL
Garlic powder	1/4 tsp.	1 mL
Paprika	1/2 tsp.	2 mL
Salt	1 tsp.	5 mL
Pepper	1/4 tsp.	1 mL

Measure flour, sugar, baking powder and salt into bowl. Stir. Add cooking oil and milk. Stir to form a soft ball. Knead dough 10 times on lightly floured surface. Line 10 x 15 inch (25 x 38 cm) jelly roll pan with waxed paper to use as a guide for size. Roll dough to fit size of pan. Pat lightly with hand to make even layer.

Combine remaining 10 ingredients in bowl. Mix. Crumble mixture over dough leaving 1/2 inch (12 mm) border all around. Use waxed paper to help roll up from longest side, removing paper as you roll. Pinch seam closed. Chill for at least 30 minutes. Cut into 1 inch (2.5 cm) slices. Arrange on greased baking sheets about 1 inch (2.5 cm) apart. Bake in 400°F (200°C) oven for 20 to 25 minutes until lightly browned. Makes 15 rolls.

1 roll: 180 Calories; 9 g Total Fat (3 g Mono, 0.5 g Poly, 2 g Sat); 20 mg Cholesterol; 17 g Carbohydrate; <1 g Fibre; 8 g Protein; 310 mg Sodium

(continued on next page)

Cinnamon Rolls: Combine 1 cup (250 mL) packed brown sugar, 1/3 cup (75 mL) all-purpose flour, 1/4 cup (60 mL) softened butter, 1 tbsp. (15 mL) cinnamon, 1 cup (250 mL) raisins and 1/2 cup (125 mL) dried cranberries in medium bowl. Sprinkle mixture over dough leaving 1/2 inch (12 mm) edges all around.

Spinach and Feta Rolls: Combine 2 1/2 cups (625 mL) chopped fresh spinach, 3/4 cup (175 mL) feta cheese and 1/4 cup (60 mL) mozzarella cheese in medium bowl. Sprinkle mixture over dough leaving 1/2 inch (12 mm) edges all around.

Egg and Cheese Burgers

A hint of spice from the hot pepper sauce makes this colourful egg burger a perfect way to kick-start your day. So satisfying, even for the heartiest of appetites. This burger tastes best fresh, but if time is an issue in the morning, you can prepare the eggs the night before and assemble the sandwich in the morning. The eggs will not be as runny if prepared in advance.

Cooking oil	1 tbsp.	15 mL
Thinly sliced onion	1 cup	250 mL
Hard margarine (or butter)	2 tsp.	10 mL
Large eggs	4	4
Cheddar cheese slices	4	4
Barbecue sauce	2 tbsp.	30 mL
Whole-wheat kaiser rolls, split and toasted (buttered, optional)	4	4
Avocado, pitted and thinly sliced	1	1
Medium tomato, thinly sliced	1	1
Hot pepper sauce	1 tsp.	5 mL

Heat cooking oil in large non-stick frying pan on medium. Add onion. Cook for 5 to 10 minutes, stirring often, until softened. Remove to small bowl. Set aside.

Melt margarine in same frying pan. Break eggs into pan. Gently break yolks. Cook eggs on medium until set. Remove from heat. Lay 1 cheese slice over each egg. Cover. Let stand until cheese is melted.

Spread barbecue sauce on bottom half of each kaiser roll and layer on avocado. Top each with 1 egg. Layer onion and tomato over eggs. Drizzle with pepper sauce. Cover each with top half of roll. Makes 4 burgers.

1 burger: 460 Calories; 25 g Total Fat (10 g Mono, 3 g Poly, 8 g Sat); 230 mg Cholesterol; 41 g Carbohydrate; 7 g Fibre; 20 g Protein; 750 mg Sodium

Chorizo Pita Pockets

Whole-wheat pita stuffed with egg, cheese and spicy Chorizo sausage. Simple but tasty. This is a really quick recipe to make, but it can be prepared the night before, if need be. Warm it in the micrwave or toaster oven when you are ready to eat.

Chorizo sausage, diced (about 3/4 cup, 175 mL)	3 3/4 oz.	106 g
Large eggs	3	3
Water	1 1/2 tbsp.	25 mL
Salt, sprinkle		
Pepper, sprinkle		
Whole-wheat pita (6 inch, 15 cm, diameter), halved crosswise	1	1
Cheddar cheese slices	2	2

Scramble-fry sausage in small non-stick frying pan on medium for about 5 minutes until golden. Remove to paper towels to drain. Remove and discard drippings from pan.

Beat eggs, water, salt and pepper with fork in small bowl until smooth. Pour egg mixture into same pan. Scramble-fry for about 1 minute until set but still creamy.

Stuff each pita with cheese, 1/2 of sausage and 1/2 of eggs. Makes 2 pockets.

1 pocket: 569 Calories; 36.6 g Total Fat (15 g Mono, 3.5 g Poly, 15 g Sat); 390 mg Cholesterol; 28 g Carbohydrate; 3 g Fibre; 32 g Protein; 1475 mg Sodium

Curried Egg Pockets

A great breakfast to eat on the run, this convenient pocket is stuffed with curried scrambled eggs, tomato, onion and cheese. Very quick and easy to prepare. If you love curry, just add a touch more.

Canola oil	1 tbsp.	15 mL
Chopped tomato	1/2 cup	125 mL
Chopped green onion	1/4 cup	60 mL
Curry powder	1 tsp.	5 mL
Large eggs, fork-beaten	6	6
Salt, sprinkle		
Pepper, sprinkle		
Whole-wheat pita bread (7 inch, 18 cm, diameter), halved and opened	2	2
Grated medium Cheddar cheese	1/2 cup	125 mL
Chopped fresh cilantro or parsley	1 tbsp.	15 mL

Heat canola oil in medium frying pan on medium. Add tomato and green onion. Cook for 2 to 3 minutes, stirring occasionally, until softened. Add curry powder. Stir. Cook for 1 minute to blend flavours.

Add eggs. Sprinkle with salt and pepper. Cook and stir until eggs are set.

Warm pita bread in microwave on high (100%) for 10 seconds. Spoon egg mixture into pita pockets. Sprinkle cheese and cilantro into pita pockets. Makes 4 pockets.

1 pocket: 258 Calories; 14.5 g Total Fat (5.4 g Mono, 2.5 g Poly, 4.6 g Sat); 289 mg Cholesterol; 18 g Carbohydrate; 3 g Fibre; 15 g Protein; 304 mg Sodium

Breakfast Pockets

These handy little pockets can be stored in the fridge for up to five days, if they last that long! When you are ready to eat, just heat them in the microwave or toaster oven until they are warmed through.

All-purpose flour	1 1/2 cups	375 mL
Natural wheat bran	2/3 cup	150 mL
Granulated sugar	1 tsp.	5 mL
Salt	1/4 tsp.	1 mL
Instant yeast	1 1/4 tsp.	6 mL
Warm water	2/3 cup	150 mL
Fancy (mild) molasses	2 tbsp.	30 mL
Cooking oil	2 tbsp.	30 mL
Bacon slices, diced	6	6
Chopped onion	1/2 cup	125 mL
Large eggs, fork-beaten	6	6
Water	3 tbsp.	45 mL
Salt	1/2 tsp.	2 mL
Pepper, sprinkle		
Hash brown potatoes	1 cup	250 mL
Ketchup	1/3 cup	75 mL
Grated part-skim mozzarella cheese (about 3 oz., 85 g)	1/2 cup	125 mL
Grated Havarti cheese (about 3 oz. 85 g)	1/2 cup	125 mL
Large egg, fork beaten	1	1
Water	1 tbsp.	15 mL

Combine first 5 ingredients in large bowl. Add next 3 ingredients. Mix well until dough leaves sides of bowl. Turn out onto lightly floured surface. Knead for 5 to 8 minutes until smooth and elastic.

Place dough in greased bowl, turning once to grease top. Cover with tea towel. Let stand in oven with light on and door closed for about 1 hour until doubled in size. Punch dough down. Split into 8 individual balls. Roll each out to about an 8 inch (20 cm) round. Set aside.

Sauté bacon and onion in frying pan until bacon is golden and onion is soft. Drain well.

(continued on next page)

Add eggs, water, salt and pepper. Heat and stir until egg is half cooked. Add hash browns and cook, stirring, for 1 minute until egg is cooked. Spread ketchup over individual crusts, using 2 tsp. each. Spoon egg mixture over half of each round.

Toss both cheeses together in small bowl. Sprinkle over filling.

Beat egg and water together. Brush edges of round with egg wash and fold dough over filling. Press down edges with fork. Brush pocket with egg wash and cut slits in top. Place on sprayed bake sheet. Bake for 20–25 minutes until cheese is melted. Makes 8 pockets.

1 pocket: 450 Calories; 27 g Total Fat (11 g Mono, 3.5 g Poly, 9 g Sat); 220 mg Cholesterol; 36 g Carbohydrate; 4 g Fibre; 16 g Protein; 760 mg Sodium

Mexican Egg Wraps

Taste buds still asleep? Wake them up with this combination of spicy salsa, Cheddar cheese and eggs nestled in a soft flour tortilla. This is just about the easiest and most delicious breakfast you can make.

Tub margarine	2 tsp.	10 mL
Large eggs	4	4
Salt, sprinkle		
Pepper, sprinkle		
Salsa	1/2 cup	125 mL
Whole-wheat flour tortillas	4	4
(6 inch, 15 cm, diameter)		
Grated light sharp Cheddar cheese	1/4 cup	60 mL
Finely chopped fresh cilantro	1 tsp.	5 mL

Melt margarine in large frying pan on medium. Break eggs, one at a time, into pan. Pierce yolks with fork. Sprinkle with salt and pepper. Cook, covered, for about 3 minutes until set.

Spread 2 tbsp. (30 mL) salsa on each tortilla, leaving 1 inch (2.5 cm) border. Place 1 egg over salsa on each tortilla. Sprinkle with cheese and cilantro. Fold sides over filling. Roll up from bottom to enclose filling. Makes 4 wraps.

1 wrap: 212 Calories; 9.1 g Total Fat (2.9 g Mono, 2.6 g Poly, 2.6 g Sat); 190 mg Cholesterol; 22 g Carbohydrate; 2 g Fibre; 11 g Protein; 486 mg Sodium

Breakfast Wraps

Colourful filling rolled inside flour tortillas. Mild bacon flavour complements the salsa and crunchy peppers. These wraps taste best when fresh, but they can be made ahead an stored in the fridge overnight if you want to save a little time in the morning. Just warm them in the microwave or toasted oven when you are ready to eat.

Bacon slices, diced	4	4
Frozen hash brown potatoes	1 cup	250 mL
Slivered green pepper	2 tbsp.	30 mL
Medium tomato, seeds removed, diced	1	1
Green onion, finely chopped	1	1
Large eggs, fork-beaten	4	4
Salt	1/8 tsp.	0.5 mL
Pepper	1/8 tsp.	0.5 mL
Flour tortillas (10 inch, 25 cm, diameter), any flavour, warmed (see Note)	4	4
Salsa	1/4 cup	60 mL

Cook bacon in large frying pan on medium until crisp. Remove to paper towels to drain. Remove drippings, reserving 1 tbsp. (15 mL) in pan. Heat reserved bacon drippings on medium-low.

Add hash brown potatoes and green pepper. Cook for about 5 minutes, stirring occasionally, until potatoes are golden and tender. Add bacon. Stir.

Add next 5 ingredients. Cook on medium-low, stirring slowly, until eggs are set.

Spread each tortilla with 1 tbsp. (15 mL) salsa. Divide and spoon egg mixture down centre of each tortilla. Fold bottom ends over filling. Fold sides in, leaving top ends open. Makes 4 wraps.

1 wrap: 312 Calories; 14.4 g Total Fat (5.9 g Mono, 2.6 g Poly, 4.5 g Sat); 224 mg Cholesterol; 33 g Carbohydrate; 3 g Fibre; 13 g Protein; 468 mg Sodium

Note: To warm tortillas, brush one side of each with water and place in a stack. Wrap the stack in foil and heat in the oven at lowest heat for 30 minutes.

Tomato, Asparagus and Egg Sandwiches

Asparagus, tomato pesto and prosciutto transform the popular egg breakfast sandwich into something divine! To save time in the morning, you could prepare the asparagus, eggs and prosciutto the night before, then toast the bread and assemble the sandwich before you head out the door in the morning.

Asparagus spears	14	14
Sundried tomato pesto	2 tbsp.	30 mL
Lime juice	1 tsp.	5 mL
Cooking oil	1 tbsp.	15 mL
Large eggs	2	2
Black pepper	1/4 tsp.	1 mL
Prosciutto slices	4	4
Whole-wheat bread slices	4	4
Light mayonnaise	2 tbsp.	30 mL

In shallow pan bring water to a boil. Add asparagus and cook for 4 minutes. Drain. Finely chop 4 asparagus spears.

Combine pesto, lime juice and asparagus. Set aside.

Heat oil in medium frying pan over medium. Add eggs and cook over easy to desired doneness. Sprinkle with pepper. Remove to plate. Add prosciutto to same frying pan and cook until crisp.

Toast bread slices.

To assemble, spread tomato mixture on 2 bread slices and mayonnaise on other 2 slices. Layer asparagus, prosciutto and eggs on tomato mixture and top with remaining bread slices. Makes 2 sandwiches.

1 sandwich: 460 Calories; 28 g Total Fat (8 g Mono, 6 g Poly, 6 g Sat); 24 mg Cholesterol; 34 g Carbohydrate; 7 g Fibre; 24 g Protein; 1120 mg Sodium

Hazelnut Pear Panini

Hazelnut spread and pear might not be a combination that springs immediately to mind, but once you've tasted it, you'll wonder why you didn't try it sooner.

Butter	2 tsp.	10 mL
Country bread slices	4	4
Hazelnut spread	3 tbsp.	45 mL
Spreadable cream cheese	2 tbsp.	30 mL
Pear, thinly sliced	1	1

Butter one side of each slice of bread.

In small bowl, combine hazelnut spread and cream cheese. Spread mixture on unbuttered side of each slice of bread. Layer pear slices on hazelnut mixture on 2 slices of bread. Top with remaining 2 slices. Cook sandwiches in panini press for 4 minutes, or place in a frying pan on medium heat and place a frying pan with weight in it on top of sandwiches. Cook for 2 minutes on each side. Makes 2 sandwiches.

1 sandwich: 370 Calories; 16 g Total Fat (4.5 g Mono, 1.5 g Poly, 6 g Sat); 30 mg Cholesterol; 54 g Carbohydrate; 5 g Fibre; 7 g Protein; 330 mg Sodium

Bacon Herb Muffins

A good breakfast muffin with an airy texture and subtle flavours. Toss one in your bag on the way out the door for an easily portable, no-mess breakfast on the go. These muffins can be stored in an airtight container for up to a week. They also freeze well and will last in the freezer for three to four months.

Bacon slices, cooked crisp and crumbled	4	4
Whole-wheat flour	1 1/4 cups	300 mL
All-purpose flour	1 1/4 cups	300 mL
Baking powder	1 tbsp.	15 mL
Salt	1/4 tsp.	1 mL
Dried sweet basil	1/2 tsp.	2 mL
Dried whole oregano	1/2 tsp.	2 mL
Grated sharp Cheddar cheese (about 4 oz., 113 g)	1 cup	250 mL
Hard margarine (or butter), melted	1/2 cup	125 mL
Large eggs, fork-beaten	2	2
Buttermilk	1 cup	250 mL
Liquid honey	1 tbsp.	15 mL

Combine first 7 ingredients in large bowl.

Add remaining 5 ingredients. Stir until just moistened. Fill greased muffin cups 3/4 full. Bake in 400°F (200°C) oven for 17 to 20 minutes until wooden pick inserted in centre comes out clean. Let stand in pan for 5 minutes. Remove to wire rack to cool. Makes 12 muffins.

1 muffin: 270 Calories; 17 g Total Fat (6 g Mono, 3.5 g Poly, 4.5 g Sat); 55 mg Cholesterol; 22 g Carbohydrate; 2 g Fibre; 8 g Protein; 370 mg Sodium

Scrambled Egg Muffins

Scrambled eggs in a handy muffin form that you can eat on the go with no worry of messing up your clothes. These muffins can be served warm or cold and can be stored in an airtight container in the fridge for up to five days.

Cooking oil	1 tbsp.	15 mL
Canadian bacon, chopped	1 1/4 cup	300 mL
Finely chopped red onion	1/2 cup	125 mL
Finely chopped green pepper	1/2 cup	125 mL
Fresh Parmesan cheese, grated	2/3 cup	150 mL
Italian seasoning	1 1/2 tsp.	7 mL
Large eggs	8	8
Milk	1/2 cup	125 mL
Salt	1/4 tsp.	1 mL
Pepper	1/4 tsp.	1 mL
Cherry tomatoes, cut in half	24	24

Heat oil in large frying pan on medium. Add bacon. Heat and stir until bacon starts to brown, about 2 minutes. Add onion and green pepper. Cook for 5 minutes, stirring often, until softened. Add cheese and Italian seasoning and cook, stirring, for 1 minute. Remove from heat and let cool. Spoon into 12 paper-lined muffin cups.

Whisk next 4 ingredients in small bowl. Pour over bacon mixture. Add 4 tomato halves to each cup. Bake in 350°F (175°C) oven for about 30 minutes until golden and set. Let stand for 5 minutes. Run knife around muffins to loosen. Remove to wire rack to cool. Makes 12 muffins.

1 muffin: 120 Calories; 6 g Total Fat (2.5 g Mono, 0.5 g Poly, 2 g Sat); 155 mg Cholesterol; 4 g Carbohydrate; <1 g Fibre; 11 g Protein; 440 mg Sodium

Frittata Muffins

Individual frittatas loaded with shrimp, peas and Parmesan cheese. Delicious!
Store in an airtight container in the fridge for up to six days.

Cooking oil	1 tbsp.	15 mL
Uncooked shrimp (peeled and deveined), coarsely chopped	3/4 lb.	340 g
Cooking oil	2 tsp.	10 mL
Finely chopped red onion	1/2 cup	125 mL
Frozen peas	1 cup	250 mL
Grated fresh Parmesan cheese	2/3 cup	150 mL
Chopped fresh mint (or 1 1/2 tsp., 7 mL, dried)	2 tbsp.	30 mL
Large eggs	8	8
Milk	1/2 cup	125 mL
Salt	1/4 tsp.	1 mL
Pepper	1/4 tsp.	1 mL

Heat first amount of cooking oil in large frying pan on medium. Add shrimp. Heat and stir until shrimp start to turn pink. Transfer to medium bowl.

Heat second amount of cooking oil in same frying pan on medium. Add onion. Cook for about 5 minutes, stirring often, until softened. Add to shrimp.

Add next 3 ingredients to shrimp mixture. Stir until well combined. Spoon shrimp mixture into 12 well-greased muffin cups.

Whisk remaining 4 ingredients in medium bowl until smooth. Pour over shrimp mixture in muffin cups. Bake in 350°F (175°C) oven for about 30 minutes until golden and set. Let stand in pan for 5 minutes. Run knife around frittatas to loosen. Remove to wire rack to cool. Serve warm or cold. Makes 12 muffins.

1 muffin: 137 Calories; 7.5 g Total Fat (3.1 g Mono, 1.3 g Poly, 2.4 g Sat); 172 mg Cholesterol; 4 g Carbohydrate; 1 g Fibre; 13 g Protein; 254 mg Sodium

Muesli Muffins

These unique muffins have no added fat or egg. For best results, do not use non-fat yogurt.

All-purpose flour	1 1/2 cups	375 mL
Baking powder	2 tsp.	10 mL
Baking soda	1/2 tsp.	2 mL
Salt	1/2 tsp.	2 mL
Ground ginger	1/2 tsp.	2 mL
Cooked oatmeal (see Note)	1 cup	250 mL
Liquid honey	1/2 cup	125 mL
Plain yogurt	1/2 cup	125 mL
Golden raisins	1/2 cup	125 mL
Chopped walnuts	1/2 cup	125 mL
Finely chopped dried apricot	1/4 cup	60 mL

Measure first 5 ingredients into large bowl. Stir. Make a well in centre.

Beat next 3 ingredients with whisk in medium bowl. Add to well.

Add remaining 3 ingredients. Stir until just moistened. Fill 12 greased muffin cups 3/4 full. Bake in 375°F (190°C) oven for 18 to 20 minutes until wooden pick inserted in centre of muffin comes out clean. Let stand in pan for 5 minutes before removing to wire rack to cool. Makes 12 muffins.

1 muffin: 197 Calories; 3.8 g Total Fat (0.9 g Mono, 2.3 g Poly, 0.4 g Sat); 1 mg Cholesterol; 39 g Carbohydrate; 2 g Fibre; 5 g Protein; 250 mg Sodium

Note: To make 1 cup (250 mL) cooked oatmeal, combine 1/2 cup (125 mL) quick-cooking rolled oats, 1/8 tsp. (0.5 mL) salt and 1 cup (250 mL) water in a small saucepan. Bring to a boil on medium. Boil gently for about 5 minutes, stirring constantly, until thickened. Cool completely before using in the muffins.

Gluten-free Chai Muffins

Wonderfully moist, fine-textured muffins filled with delicious, aromatic spices.

White (or brown) rice flour	1 1/2 cups	375 mL
Soy flour	1/2 cup	125 mL
Gluten-free baking powder (see Tip, below)	1 tsp.	5 mL
Baking soda	1 tsp.	5 mL
Ground cinnamon	1 tsp.	5 mL
Salt	1/2 tsp.	2 mL
Ground allspice	1/4 tsp.	1 mL
Ground nutmeg	1/4 tsp.	1 mL
Ground cardamom (optional)	1/4 tsp.	1 mL
Large eggs	2	2
Chai tea concentrate	3/4 cup	175 mL
Liquid honey	1/2 cup	125 mL
Cooking oil	1/4 cup	60 mL
Unsweetened applesauce	1/4 cup	60 mL
Vanilla yogurt	1/4 cup	60 mL

Measure first 9 ingredients into large bowl. Stir. Make a well in centre.

Combine remaining 6 ingredients in medium bowl. Add to well. Stir until just moistened. Batter will be thin. Fill 12 greased muffin cups 3/4 full. Bake in 375°F (190°C) oven for about 20 minutes until wooden pick inserted in centre of muffin comes out clean. Let stand in pan for 5 minutes before removing to wire rack to cool. Makes 12 muffins.

1 muffin: 215 Calories; 6.9 g Total Fat (3.5 g Mono, 2.1 g Poly, 0.9 g Sat); 36 mg Cholesterol; 36 g Carbohydrate; 1 g Fibre; 4 g Protein; 252 mg Sodium

Tip: You can buy gluten-free baking powder, or you can make your own. To make 1 tbsp. (15 mL) gluten-free baking powder, combine 2 tsp. (10 mL) cream of tartar and 1 tsp. (5 mL) baking soda. Store any remaining baking powder in an airtight container.

"Free" Muffins

Dairy free, egg free, gluten free and delicious! The rice flour adds a grainy texture to these flavourful muffins.

White (or brown) rice flour	1 1/2 cups	375 mL
Soy flour	1/2 cup	125 mL
Gluten-free baking powder (see Tip, page 34)	2 tsp.	10 mL
Ground cinnamon	1 tsp.	5 mL
Baking soda	1/2 tsp.	2 mL
Ground allspice	1/4 tsp.	1 mL
Salt	1/4 tsp.	1 mL
Ground flaxseed (see Tip, page 48)	1 tbsp.	15 mL
Water	3 tbsp.	45 mL
Unsweetened applesauce	1 cup	250 mL
Brown sugar, packed	1/2 cup	125 mL
Cooking oil	1/4 cup	60 mL
Vanilla extract	1 tsp.	5 mL
Medium cooking apples (such as McIntosh), peeled and diced	2	2
Chopped pecans	1/2 cup	125 mL
TOPPING		
Chopped pecans	1/4 cup	60 mL
Brown sugar, packed	3 tbsp.	45 mL
Soy flour	1 tbsp.	15 mL
Cooking oil	1 tbsp.	15 mL

Measure first 7 ingredients into large bowl. Stir. Make a well in centre.

Process ground flaxseed and water in blender for about 1 minute until smooth. Add next 4 ingredients. Process until smooth. Add to well. Add apple and pecans. Stir until just moistened. Fill 12 greased muffin cups 3/4 full.

Topping: Combine all 4 ingredients in small bowl. Sprinkle on batter. Bake in 375°F (190°C) oven for about 20 minutes until wooden pick inserted in centre of muffin comes out clean. Let stand in pan for 5 minutes before removing to wire rack to cool. Makes 12 muffins.

1 muffin: 277 Calories; 12.8 g Total Fat (7.2 g Mono, 3.9 g Poly, 1.1 g Sat); 0 mg Cholesterol; 39 g Carbohydrate; 2 g Fibre; 4 g Protein; 172 mg Sodium

Apple Streusel Muffins

These dense muffins have no wheat or dairy, making them a good choice for people with allergies or intolerances. They will fill you up and keep you going all morning long.

White rice flour	1 1/2 cups	375 mL
Oat flour (see Note)	1 cup	250 mL
Agave syrup	1/2 cup	125 mL
Baking powder	2 tsp.	10 mL
Baking soda	1/2 tsp.	2 mL
Salt	1/2 tsp.	2 mL
Ground cinnamon	1/2 tsp.	2 mL
Ground nutmeg	1/4 tsp.	1 mL
Large eggs	2	2
Unsweetened applesauce	1 cup	250 mL
Cooking oil	1/4 cup	60 mL
Finely chopped peeled cooking apple (such as McIntosh)	1/2 cup	125 mL
Chopped walnuts (or pecans)	1/2 cup	125 mL
TOPPING		
Finely chopped walnuts	1/4 cup	60 mL
Oat flour (see Note)	2 tbsp.	30 mL
Brown sugar	1 tsp.	5 mL
Ground cinnamon	1/4 tsp.	1 mL

Measure first 8 ingredients into large bowl. Stir. Make a well in centre.

Combine next 3 ingredients in medium bowl. Add to well.

Add apple and walnuts. Stir until just moistened. Fill 12 greased muffin cups 3/4 full.

Topping: Combine all 4 ingredients in small bowl. Sprinkle on batter. Bake in 375°F (190°C) oven for 18 to 20 minutes until wooden pick inserted in centre of muffin comes out clean. Let stand in pan for 5 minutes before removing to wire rack to cool. Makes 12 muffins.

1 muffin: 270 Calories; 11 g Total Fat (3.5 g Mono, 4.5 g Poly, 1.5 g Sat); 35 mg Cholesterol; 40 g Carbohydrate; 2 g Fibre; 4 g Protein; 210 mg Sodium

Note: To make 1 cup (250 mL) plus 2 tbsp. (30 mL) oat flour, process 1 1/4 cups (300 mL) quick-cooking rolled oats in a blender or food processor until finely ground.

Spiced Sweet Potato Muffins

These fragrant, pleasantly spiced sweet potato muffins are also filled with the goodness of bran—but no one will know unless you tell them! Moist and packed with flavour.

All-purpose flour	2 cups	500 mL
Granulated sugar	1/2 cup	125 mL
Natural wheat bran	1/2 cup	125 mL
Baking powder	2 tsp.	10 mL
Baking soda	1/2 tsp.	2 mL
Ground cinnamon	1/2 tsp.	2 mL
Salt	1/2 tsp.	2 mL
Ground ginger	1/4 tsp.	1 mL
Ground nutmeg	1/4 tsp.	1 mL
Ground cloves	1/8 tsp.	0.5 mL
Large eggs, fork-beaten	2	2
Mashed peeled orange-fleshed sweet potato (about 3/4 lb., 340 g, uncooked)	1 cup	250 mL
Buttermilk (or soured milk, see Tip, below)	2/3 cup	150 mL
Cooking oil	1/4 cup	60 mL

Combine first 10 ingredients in large bowl. Make a well in centre.

Combine remaining 4 ingredients in small bowl. Add to well. Stir until just moistened. Fill 12 greased muffin cups 3/4 full. Bake in 375°F (190°C) oven for about 20 minutes until wooden pick inserted in centre of muffin comes out clean. Let stand in pan for 5 minutes before removing to wire rack to cool. Makes 12 muffins.

1 muffin: 176 Calories; 5.8 g Total Fat (3.2 g Mono, 1.5 g Poly, 0.8 g Sat); 36 mg Cholesterol; 29 g Carbohydrate; 2 g Fibre; 4 g Protein; 272 mg Sodium

Tip: To make soured milk, measure 1 tbsp. (15 mL) white vinegar or lemon juice into a 1 cup (250 mL) liquid measure. Add enough milk to make 1 cup (250 mL). Stir. Let stand for 1 minute.

Quinoa Cranberry Muffins

These nutritious muffins are ideal to serve up for breakfast, with their pleasant quinoa crunch and sweet bits of cranberry. Healthy never tasted so good!

Water	3/4 cup	175 mL
Salt	1/8 tsp.	0.5 mL
Quinoa, rinsed and drained	1/2 cup	125 mL
All-purpose flour	1 cup	250 mL
Whole-wheat flour	1 cup	250 mL
Brown sugar, packed	1/3 cup	75 mL
Baking powder	1 1/2 tsp.	7 mL
Salt	3/4 tsp.	4 mL
Baking soda	1/4 tsp.	1 mL
Large egg	1	1
Buttermilk (or soured milk, see Tip, page 42)	1 1/4 cups	300 mL
Applesauce	1/3 cup	75 mL
Cooking oil	1/4 cup	60 mL
Dried cranberries, chopped	1 1/4 cups	300 mL

Combine water and salt in small saucepan. Bring to a boil. Add quinoa. Stir. Reduce heat to medium-low. Simmer, covered, for about 20 minutes, without stirring, until quinoa is tender and liquid is absorbed. Transfer to small bowl. Cool completely.

Combine next 6 ingredients in large bowl. Make a well in centre.

Whisk next 4 ingredients in medium bowl.

Add cranberries and quinoa. Stir. Add to well. Stir until just moistened. Fill 12 greased muffin cups full. Bake in 375°F (190°C) oven for about 30 minutes until wooden pick inserted in centre of muffin comes out clean. Let stand in pan for 5 minutes before removing to wire rack to cool. Makes 12 muffins.

1 muffin: 220 Calories; 6.2 g Total Fat (3.2 g Mono, 1.7 g Poly, 0.9 g Sat); 20 mg Cholesterol; 38 g Carbohydrate; 3 g Fibre; 5 g Protein; 272 mg Sodium

Avocado Banana Bread

Banana bread gets a heart-healthy makeover by replacing the traditional butter or shortening with avocado. The result is a super-moist loaf with a subtle banana flavour. So good!

Old-fashioned oats	1/3 cup	75 mL
All-purpose flour	1 cup	250 mL
Baking powder	1 tsp.	5 mL
Baking soda	1 tsp.	5 mL
Ground cinnamon	1 tsp.	5 mL
Ripe avocado, seeded	1	1
Brown sugar, packed	1 cup	250 mL
Large eggs	2	2
Ripe banana	1	1
Chopped walnuts	1/2 cup	125 mL
Almond milk	1/4 cup	60 mL

Combine oats, flour, baking powder, baking soda and cinnamon in medium bowl. Set aside.

Scoop avocado into large bowl and mash lightly. Add brown sugar and cream together using electric mixer until light and creamy.

Add eggs, one at a time, beating well after each addition.

Add banana. Stir. Add walnuts. Stir. Add dry ingredients. Stir in almond milk until just incorporated. Pour into 9 x 5 x 3 inch (23 x 12.5 x 7.5 cm) loaf pan lined with foil and bake in 350°F (175°C) oven for about 1 hour. If top is becoming too brown, cover with foil around the 45 minute mark. Bread is cooked when top bounces back when lightly pushed (see Tip, below). Loaf cuts into 16 slices.

1 slice: 150 Calories; 5 g Total Fat (2 g Mono, 2 g Poly, 0.5 g Sat); 25 mg Cholesterol; 24 g Carbohydrate; 2 g Fibre; 3 g Protein; 115 mg Sodium

Tip: This bread is so moist that the toothpick test generally does not work—even once the bread is fully cooked, a toothpick inserted in the middle will not come out clean. To check for doneness, gently push the top of the loaf with your fingertip; the bread will spring back when it is fully cooked.

Breakfast Bars

These dense, nutrient-packed bars are perfect for a breakfast on the run or a quick pick-me-up during the day.

All-purpose flour	1 1/2 cups	375 mL
Natural oat bran	1/2 cup	125 mL
Granulated sugar	3/4 cup	175 mL
Baking powder	1 tbsp.	15 mL
Salt	1/2 tsp.	2 mL
Large eggs	2	2
Butter, melted	1/4 cup	60 mL
Milk	1 cup	250 mL
Blueberries	1 cup	250 mL
Chopped pitted dates	1 cup	250 mL
Chopped walnuts, toasted (see Tip, page 52)	1 cup	250 mL

Combine first 5 ingredients in large bowl. Make a well in centre.

Combine next 3 ingredients in small bowl. Add to well.

Add remaining 3 ingredients. Stir just until moistened. Spread in greased 9 x 13 inch (23 x 33 cm) pan. Bake in 350°F (175°C) oven for 35 minutes until wooden pick inserted in centre comes out clean. Cuts into 20 bars.

1 bar: 170 Calories; 7 g Total Fat (1.5 g Mono, 3 g Poly, 2 g Sat); 30 mg Cholesterol; 26 g Carbohydrate; 2 g Fibre; 4 g Protein; 135 mg Sodium

Blackberry Cereal Bars

Blackberries pack a nutritional wallop and are loaded with antioxidants, vitamins and fibre, an excellent reason to add them to your breakfast routine. If you aren't really a blackberry fan, feel free to substitute the berry of your preference—raspberries, strawberries, saskatoons and blueberries would all work just as well.

Whole-wheat flour	1 1/2 cups	375 mL
Rolled oats	1 1/2 cups	375 mL
Brown sugar, firmly packed	1/2 cup	125 mL
Ground flax seed (see Tip, below)	1/2 cup	125 mL
Ground cinnamon	1 tsp.	5 mL
Baking soda	1/2 tsp.	2 mL
Salt	1/4 tsp.	1 mL
Butter, cut up	1 cup	250 mL
Blackberries	2 cups	500 mL
Sugar	1/3 cup	75 mL
Whole-wheat flour	1 tbsp.	15 mL
Vanilla extract	1 tsp.	5 mL
Lemon juice	1 tbsp.	15 mL

In a large bowl, combine first 7 ingredients. Cut in butter until mixture resembles coarse crumbs. Press half of mixture into a 9 x 13 inch (23 x 33 cm) baking dish sprayed with cooking spray. Set remaining mixture aside.

Combine remaining 5 ingredients in blender and process until smooth. Spread over mixture in pan. Sprinkle remaining flour mixture over top. Bake in 350°F (175°C) oven for 25 to 30 minutes until top begins to brown. Cool completely before slicing. Cuts into 12 bars. Store in an airtight container for up to a week, or freeze for three to four months.

1 bar: 320 Calories; 18 g Total Fat (4.5 g Mono, 2 g Poly, 10 g Sat); 40 mg Cholesterol; 37 g Carbohydrate; 6 g Fibre; 5 g Protein; 210 mg Sodium

Tip: To make 1/4 cup (60 mL) ground flaxseed, grind 2 1/2 tbsp. (37 mL) whole flaxseed in a blender or coffee grinder. Store in airtight container in the refrigerator.

Ground flaxseed is digested more readily than whole flaxseeds, which simply pass through the body. Grinding the seeds just before using them best preserves flavour and nutrients, but pre-ground seeds are more convenient.

Breakfast Bites

Cookies for breakfast? Not quite, but these bites are quick, easy to make and healthy whether eaten as a breakfast, a dessert or a snack.

Large egg, fork-beaten	1	1
Overripe medium banana, mashed	1	1
Grated carrot	1 cup	250 mL
Sliced natural almonds, toasted (see Tip, below)	1/2 cup	125 mL
Brown sugar, packed	1/2 cup	125 mL
Unsweetened applesauce	1/4 cup	60 mL
Vanilla extract	1/4 tsp.	1 mL
Whole-wheat flour	1 cup	250 mL
Quick-cooking rolled oats	1/2 cup	125 mL
Flaxseed	1/4 cup	60 mL
Baking soda	1/2 tsp.	2 mL
Salt	1/2 tsp.	2 mL
Ground cinnamon	1/4 tsp.	1 mL

Combine first 7 ingredients in large bowl.

Add remaining 6 ingredients. Stir until no dry flour remains. Drop by rounded tablespoonfuls about 1 inch (2.5 cm) apart onto greased cookie sheet. Bake in 350°F (175°C) oven for about 12 minutes until set and bottoms are browned. Remove bites from cookie sheet and place on wire rack to cool. Makes 24 bites. Store in an airtight container for up to a week, or freeze for up to three months.

1 bite: 74 Calories; 2.2 g Total Fat (0.9 g Mono, 0.9 g Poly, 0.2 g Sat); 8 mg Cholesterol; 12 g Carbohydrate; 2 g Fibre; 2 g Protein; 84 mg Sodium

Tip: When toasting nuts, seeds or coconut, cooking times will vary for each type of nut—so never toast them together. To toast nuts, seeds or coconut, place them in an ungreased shallow frying pan. Heat on medium for 3 to 5 minutes, stirring often, until golden. To bake, spread them evenly in an ungreased shallow pan. Bake in a 350°F (175°C) oven for 5 to 10 minutes, stirring or shaking often, until golden.

Healthy Banana Cookies

No need to feel guilty about eating these cookies for breakfast! With no added fat or sugar, these moist morsels are more like a solid, hand-held bowl of oatmeal than a cookie. Oats, walnuts, dates, banana—there is not one unhealthy ingredient in the mix!

Ripe bananas	3	3
Rolled oats	2 cups	500 mL
Dates, pitted and chopped	1 cup	250 mL
Unsweetened applesauce	1/3 cup	75 mL
Vanilla extract	1 tsp.	5 mL
Ground cinnamon	1 tsp.	5 mL
Chopped walnuts	1/4 cup	60 mL
Dried cranberries (optional)	1/2 cup	125 mL

Mash bananas in large bowl. Stir in oats, dates, applesauce, vanilla, cinnamon, walnuts and cranberries. Mix well, and allow to sit for 15 minutes. Drop by teaspoonfuls onto an ungreased cookie sheet. Bake in 350°F (175°C) oven for about 20 minutes, until lightly brown. Makes 14 cookies. Store in an airtight container for up to a week, or freeze for up to three months.

1 cookie: 120 Calories; 2.5 g Total Fat (0 g Mono, 1.5 g Poly, 0 g Sat); 0 mg Cholesterol; 24 g Carbohydrate; 3 g Fibre; 2 g Protein; 0 mg Sodium

Oatmeal Packets

A homemade version of the popular commercial instant oatmeal packages. Simple and inexpensive, but oh so tasty!

Quick-cooking rolled oats	1/2 cup	125 mL
Non-fat milk powder	1 tsp.	5 mL
Brown sugar	2 tsp.	10 mL
Ground cinnamon	1/2 tsp.	2 mL
Ground nutmeg	1/2 tsp.	2 mL

Combine all ingredients in a small resealable plastic bag. To serve, pour contents of oatmeal packets into bowl and add 1 to 1 1/4 cups (250 to 300 mL) boiling water. Stir for 20 to 30 seconds. Add more water as necessary for desired consistency.

1 serving: 190 Calories; 3 g Total Fat (1 g Mono, 1 g Poly, 0.5 g Sat); 0 mg Cholesterol; 37 g Carbohydrate; 4 g Fibre; 6 g Protein; 10 mg Sodium

Apple Walnut: Add 3 tbsp. (45 mL) chopped dried apple and 2 tbsp. (30 mL) chopped walnuts.

Cherry Spice: Add 3 tbsp. (45 mL) dried cherries and replace cinnamon with 1/4 tsp. (1 mL) ground ginger.

Triple Berry: Add 2 tbsp. (30 mL) each dried blueberries, dried chopped cranberries and dried chopped strawberries. Replace nutmeg with 1/4 tsp (1 mL) ground ginger.

Tropical Cream: Add 2 tbsp. (30 mL) each dried chopped mango, dried papaya and dried pinapple, as well as 1/4 cup (60 mL) half-and-half cream.

Cheese and Honey

A soft whey cheese, such as Manouri or Manoypi, is often served like this for breakfast in Greece. We tried it with readily available low-fat quark cheese for a delicious and almost authentic alternative. Pairs well with fresh berries or sliced fruit.

Liquid honey	**2 tbsp.**	**30 mL**
Low-fat quark cheese	**1/3 cup**	**75 mL**
Coarsely chopped walnuts (optional)	**2 tsp.**	**10 mL**
Ground cinnamon, sprinkle (optional)		

Drizzle honey over cheese in small portable dish with tight-fitting lid. Stir gently just to marble honey through cheese. Sprinkle with walnuts and cinnamon, if using. Serves 1.

1 serving: 250 Calories; 8 Total Fat (1.5 g Mono, 2.5 g Poly, 3 g Sat); 15 mg Cholesterol; 45 g Carbohydrate; 0 g Fibre; 4 g Protein; 40 mg Sodium

Tropical Fruit Salad

This fruit salad makes a nice light breakfast but still provides a dose of protein to keep you going until your next meal. Just scoop it into a container with a tight-fitting lid and toss it into your bag before you head out the door in the morning.

Plain non-fat yogurt	1 cup	250 mL
Agave syrup	1 tbsp.	15 mL
Chopped fresh mint	1 tbsp.	15 mL
Ground nutmeg, pinch		
Kiwi, peeled, quartered and chopped	2	2
Medium papaya, peeled, seeded and chopped	1	1
Mango, peeled and chopped	1	1
Chopped watermelon	1 cup	250 mL
Fresh pineapple chunks	1 cup	250 mL
Brazil nuts, chopped	1/2 cup	125 mL
Medium sweetened coconut, toasted (see Tip, page 50)	1 tbsp.	15 mL
Bananas	2	2
Lemon juice	2 tsp.	10 mL

Combine first 4 ingredients in small bowl. Set aside.

In large bowl, combine next 7 ingredients. In separate bowl, combine bananas and lemon juice. Add to fruit mixture. Top individual servings with dollop of yogurt mixture. Store fruit salad and yogurt mixture separately in fridge for up to 2 days. Serves 6.

1 serving: 230 Calories; 9 g Total Fat (3 g Mono, 2.5 g Poly, 2.5 g Sat); 0 mg Cholesterol; 38 g Carbohydrate; 5 g Fibre; 5 g Protein; 35 mg Sodium

Green Chill

Sweet and delicious. A great way to sneak a bit of spinach into your diet—the sweetness of the fruit masks the spinach, but you still reap the nutritional benefits!

Vanilla soy milk	1 1/2 cups	375 mL
Frozen pineapple chunks	1/2 cup	125 mL
Apple chunks, peel on	1/2 cup	125 mL
Chopped spinach	1/2 cup	125 mL
Agave syrup (see Note, below)	1 tbsp.	15 mL
Apple juice	1/4 cup	60 mL

Combine first 5 ingredients in blender. Process until smooth, adding apple juice if the mixture is too thick. Serves 2.

1 serving: 170 Calories; 3 g Total Fat (1 g Mono, 1.5 g Poly, 0 g Sat); 0 mg Cholesterol; 30 g Carbohydrate; 3 g Fibre; 6 g Protein; 250 mg Sodium

Note: Agave nectar, also called agave syrup, is made from the sap of several species of agave plant, including blue agave *(Agave tequilana)*, the same species that gives us tequila. It is used as a sweetener and can be a healthier alternative to sugar or other highly processed sweeteners like corn syrup. Agave nectar is sweeter than sugar and can have more calories, depending on the manufacturer, but because it is so sweet, a little goes a long way. It is made primarily of a type of fructose called inulin, which does not cause the spike in blood sugar levels that is seen with sugar.

Apricot Breakfast Drink

Golden and creamy, with a frothy layer on top. A satisfying start to your morning!

Can of apricot halves in light syrup (with syrup)	14 oz.	398 mL
Ice cubes	16	16
Milk	1 cup	250 mL
Low-fat plain yogurt	1/2 cup	125 mL
Liquid honey (see Tip, below)	2 tbsp.	30 mL
Ground nutmeg	1/8 tsp.	0.5 mL

Process all 6 ingredients in blender until smooth. Makes about 5 cups (1.25 L). Pour into 3 large glasses. Serves 3.

1 serving: 173 Calories; 1.1 g Total Fat (0.3 g Mono, 0.1 g Poly, 0.6 g Sat); 4 mg Cholesterol; 38 g Carbohydrate; 1 g Fibre; 6 g Protein; 79 mg Sodium

Tip: When measuring sticky ingredients like honey or nut butters, first lightly oil your measuring cups or spoons to help the ingredient slide right out.

Tropical Soy Shake

Shake up your day with this pineapple smoothie. Pineapple is an excellent source of vitamin C, helps promote healthy digestion, strengthens the immune system and is even believed to help reduce stress. What better way to start the day!

Can of pineapple chunks (with juice)	14 oz.	398 mL
Soy milk	1 cup	250 mL
Frozen overripe medium banana	1	1
(see Tip, page 82)		
Ice cubes	4	4
Ground nutmeg, sprinkle (optional)		

Process all 5 ingredients in blender until smooth. Makes about 4 cups (1 L). Pour into 4 medium glasses. Serves 4.

1 serving: 110 Calories; 1.4 g Total Fat (0.2 g Mono, 0.6 g Poly, 0.2 g Sat); 0 mg Cholesterol; 24 g Carbohydrate; 2 g Fibre; 2 g Protein; 9 mg Sodium

Very Berry Frappé

Berry lovers will rejoice at this bold, refreshing, zesty smoothie. Loaded with protein, it will keep you going all morning long.

Frozen mixed berries	2 cups	500 mL
Milk (or soy milk)	1 cup	250 mL
Dessert tofu (such as Pete's Tofu Very Berry-flavoured dessert), or plain soft tofu (see Note, below)	3/4 cup	175 mL
Cranberry cocktail	1/2 cup	125 mL
Liquid honey	1 tbsp.	15 mL

Process all 5 ingredients in blender until smooth. Makes about 3 1/4 cups (800 mL). Pour into 2 large glasses. Serves 2.

1 serving: 277 Calories; 6.5 g Total Fat (1.4 g Mono, 2.7 g Poly, 1.5 g Sat); 5 mg Cholesterol; 47 g Carbohydrate; 7 g Fibre; 13 g Protein; 75 mg Sodium

Note: What's dessert tofu? Tofu comes in several varieties that differ in firmness, the softest of which is called silken tofu. This type has the highest moisture content and a fine, soft, custard-like texture. Dessert tofu is very much like silken tofu, but with different flavours and sweeteners added to it. You can add it to recipes or eat it as a snack on its own.

Yogurt Fruit Smoothie

Very sweet, very pretty beverage with a whisper of cinnamon. Even dedicated late-sleepers will happily get out of bed knowing this smoothie is on the breakfast menu.

Fresh strawberries	8	8
Ripe medium banana, cut up (see Tip, page 82)	1	1
Vanilla yogurt	1 1/2 cups	375 mL
Frozen blueberries	1/2 cup	125 mL
Frozen concentrated orange juice	2 tbsp.	30 mL
Ground cinnamon	1/8 tsp.	0.5 mL
Ice cubes	3	3

Process all 7 ingredients in blender until smooth. Makes about 3 3/4 cups (925 mL). Pour into 4 small glasses. Serves 4.

1 serving: 149 Calories; 2.3 g Total Fat (0.5 g Mono, 0.1 g Poly, 1.3 g Sat); 5 mg Cholesterol; 30 g Carbohydrate; 2 g Fibre; 5 g Protein; 57 mg Sodium

Paradise Smoothie

Jump-start your morning with a taste of paradise—beverage style! Tasty tropical flavours of coconut, pineapple and banana are sure to get you on your way. Chill the can of crushed pineapple to make it even more refreshing.

Frozen overripe medium banana (see Tip, page 82)	1	1
Can of crushed pineapple (with juice)	14 oz.	398 mL
Vanilla frozen yogurt	1 cup	250 mL
Light silken tofu (about 3/4 cup, 175 mL)	6 oz.	170 g
Sliced natural almonds	1 tbsp.	15 mL
Medium unsweetened coconut	1 tbsp.	15 mL

Combine all 6 ingredients in blender. Process with on/off motion until almonds are broken up. Blend until smooth. Makes about 3 1/4 cups (800 mL). Serves 2.

1 serving: 375 Calories; 8.4 g Total Fat (1.1 g Mono, 0.8 g Poly, 4.6 g Sat); 15 mg Cholesterol; 65 g Carbohydrate; 4 g Fibre; 10 g Protein; 136 mg Sodium

PBAJ Smoothie

Peanut butter, amaranth and jam would be good in a sandwich but are splendid in a smoothie.

Amaranth, toasted (see Tip, below)	3 tbsp.	45 mL
Milk	1 cup	250 mL
Vanilla yogurt	1/2 cup	125 mL
Smooth peanut butter	1/4 cup	60 mL
Raspberry jam	3 tbsp.	45 mL

Put amaranth into blender. Process until finely ground.

Add remaining 4 ingredients. Process until smooth. Makes about 2 cups (500 mL).

1 cup (250 mL): 436 Calories; 19.8 g Total Fat (8.4 g Mono, 5.0 g Poly, 4.9 g Sat); 8 mg Cholesterol; 52 g Carbohydrate; 4 g Fibre; 17 g Protein; 104 mg Sodium

Tip: To toast grains, put them in a shallow frying pan. Heat on medium for about 5 minutes, stirring often, until golden. Remember not to toast more than one type of grain at a time because some types may take longer to toast than others.

Mango Tango

Get your morning energy boost in a convenient beverage! Using frozen fruit helps to thicken and chill smoothies. For a more intense mango flavour, use mango nectar or mango-peach fruit cocktail instead of orange juice.

Frozen mango pieces	2 cups	500 mL
Milk (or soy milk)	1 cup	250 mL
Peach (or peach-mango) dessert tofu	5 1/3 oz.	150 g
Orange juice	1/2 cup	125 mL
Wheat germ, toasted (see Tip, below)	1 tbsp.	15 mL

Process all 5 ingredients in blender until smooth. Makes 3 1/2 cups (875 mL). Serves 2.

1 serving: 254 Calories; 3.5 g Total Fat (0.7 g Mono, 0.3 g Poly, 1.1 g Sat); 8 mg Cholesterol; 52 g Carbohydrate; 4 g Fibre; 9 g Protein; 74 mg Sodium

Tip: To toast wheat germ, spread evenly in an ungreased frying pan. Heat and stir on medium until golden. To bake, spread evenly in an ungreased shallow pan. Bake in a 350°F (175°C) oven for 3 minutes, stirring or shaking often, until golden. Cool before adding to recipe.

Razzle-dazzle Smoothie

The addition of chocolate makes this raspberry smoothie dazzle! Forget fat-filled milkshakes—this nutritious beverage is the best way to get your next chocolate fix.

Frozen whole raspberries	2 cups	500 mL
Non-fat raspberry yogurt	2 cups	500 mL
Light hot chocolate mix	1/2 cup	125 mL
Skim milk	1/2 cup	125 mL
Large banana, sliced	1	1
Ice cubes	8	8

Process all 6 ingredients in blender or food processor until smooth. Makes about 5 cups (1.25 L). Serves 4.

1 serving: 230 Calories; 0.7 g Total Fat (trace Mono, trace Poly, 0.1 g Sat); 3 mg Cholesterol; 43 g Carbohydrate; 7 g Fibre; 13 g Protein; 534 mg Sodium

Berry Bran Shake

Breakfast in a glass! The natural sweetness of fruit gets a boost from raisin bran to make a winning breakfast beverage.

Frozen whole strawberries, cut up	2 cups	500 mL
Milk	2 cups	500 mL
Raisin bran cereal	1/2 cup	125 mL
Chopped pitted dates (see Tip, below)	1/4 cup	60 mL

Process all 4 ingredients in blender or food processor for about 3 minutes until smooth. Makes about 4 cups (1 L).

1 cup (250 mL): 132 Calories; 1.8 g Total Fat (0.4 g Mono, 0.2 g Poly, 0.9 g Sat); 5 mg Cholesterol; 26 g Carbohydrate; 4 g Fibre; 5 g Protein; 109 mg Sodium

Tip: Cutting dates with a knife can be a nuisance, but a good pair of kitchen shears makes light work of the task. Dip the blades of the shears in hot water to keep the fruit from sticking.

Strawberry Carrot Smoothie

Get your morning off to a good start with this thick, creamy and not-too-sweet smoothie. You could cook extra carrots at dinnertime so you're all ready to go in the morning.

Chopped carrot	2 cups	500 mL
Frozen overripe medium banana, cut up (see Tip, below)	1	1
Whole frozen strawberries	1 cup	250 mL
Milk	3/4 cup	175 mL
Vanilla yogurt	3/4 cup	175 mL
Liquid honey	2 tsp.	10 mL

Pour water into small saucepan until about 1 inch (2.5 cm) deep. Add carrot. Cover. Bring to a boil. Reduce heat to medium. Boil gently for about 10 minutes until tender. Drain. Plunge into ice water in medium bowl. Let stand for about 10 minutes until cold. Drain. Transfer to blender or food processor.

Add remaining 5 ingredients. Process until smooth. Makes about 3 1/2 cups (875 mL). Serves 4.

1 serving: 130 Calories; 2.5 g Total Fat (0 g Mono, 0 g Poly, 1 g Sat); 5 mg Cholesterol; 26 g Carbohydrate; 3 g Fibre; 5 g Protein; 105 mg Sodium

Tip: When your bananas get too ripe to enjoy fresh, peel and cut them into 2 inch (5 cm) chunks and arrange in a single layer on a baking sheet. Freeze until firm. Store in a resealable freezer bag. Use 4 pieces for 1 medium banana.

Morning Burritos

A great breakfast for the whole family. Serve with fresh fruit.

Chopped green onion	1/4 cup	60 mL
Margarine	2 tsp.	10 mL
Frozen egg product, thawed (see Note)	1 cup	250 mL
Chili powder	1/4 tsp.	1 mL
Salt	1/4 tsp.	1 mL
Chopped pickled hot peppers	2 tbsp.	30 mL
Grated light sharp Cheddar cheese	3/4 cup	175 mL
Whole-wheat flour tortillas (10 inch, 25 cm, size), warmed	4	4
Salsa (optional)	2 tbsp.	30 mL
Light sour cream (optional)	2 tbsp.	30 mL

Sauté green onion in margarine in large non-stick frying pan for about 30 seconds. Pour in egg product. Sprinkle with chili powder and salt. Heat, stirring occasionally, on medium until egg starts to set. Add peppers. Heat until egg is cooked.

Divide and sprinkle cheese over tortillas. Place 1/4 of egg mixture in line down centre of each tortilla over cheese. Top egg mixture with salsa and sour cream. Roll tortillas, tucking in sides, to enclose filling. Cut in half to serve. Makes 4 burritos.

1 burrito: 300 Calories; 11 g Total Fat (1 g Mono, 1 g Poly, 4 g Sat); 15 mg Cholesterol; 33 g Carbohydrate; 4 g Fibre; 11 g Protein; 1040 mg Sodium

Note: With frozen egg product, 3 tbsp. (45 mL) is equal to 1 large egg.

Egg and Pepper Burritos

Delicious tortillas filled with scrambled eggs and topped with chunky salsa and cheese.

Cooking oil	1 tbsp.	15 mL
Chopped green onion	1/4 cup	60 mL
Finely chopped red pepper	1/2 cup	125 mL
Finely chopped green pepper	1/2 cup	125 mL
Large eggs	8	8
Milk	2 tbsp.	30 mL
Hot pepper sauce	1 tsp.	5 mL
Salt	1/4 tsp.	1 mL
Flour tortillas (8 inch, 20 cm, diameter)	4	4
Salsa	1/2 cup	125 mL
Grated medium Cheddar cheese	3/4 cup	175 mL

Heat cooking oil in large frying pan on medium. Add next 3 ingredients. Cook for about 5 minutes, stirring often, until peppers are softened.

Stir next 4 ingredients with whisk in medium bowl until well combined. Pour into frying pan. Cook for 2 to 3 minutes, stirring occasionally, until eggs are almost set. Remove from heat. Makes 2 2/3 cups (650 mL) filling.

Divide and spoon egg mixture down centre of each tortilla. Roll up tightly to enclose filling. Secure with wooden picks if necessary. Place on well-greased baking sheet with sides.

Spoon salsa on top of each burrito and sprinkle with cheese. Broil 5 inches (12.5 cm) from heat for about 3 minutes until cheese is melted and tops of tortillas are golden. For crispier burritos, bake in 375°F (190°C) oven for about 10 minutes until slightly crisp and golden. Makes 4 burritos.

1 burrito: 407 Calories; 23.7 g Total Fat (9 g Mono, 3.7 g Poly, 8.5 g Sat); 455 mg Cholesterol; 26 g Carbohydrate; 2 g Fibre; 22 g Protein; 676 mg Sodium

G' Morning Pizza

This tasty pizza was a huge hit in our test kitchen—it disappeared in less than five minutes! A breakfast the whole family will enjoy, this dish is easy and quick to prepare. It is also a good choice for diabetics.

Large hard-boiled eggs, peeled	6	6
Light cream cheese	4 oz.	125 g
Parsley flakes	1/2 tsp.	2 mL
Dried sweet basil	1/2 tsp.	2 mL
Garlic powder	1/16 tsp.	0.5 mL
Premade pizza crust, 12 inch (30 cm)	1	1
Fat-free ham slices, diced	2/3 cup	150 mL
Grated part-skim mozzarella cheese	1 cup	250 mL
Thinly sliced red onion	1/2 cup	125 mL
Thinly sliced green and red peppers	2/3 cup	150 mL
Dried sweet basil, sprinkle (optional)		
Dried whole oregano, sprinkle (optional)		

Discard 4 yolks or set aside to use in another recipe. Chop remaining egg whites and 2 whole eggs.

Combine next 4 ingredients in small bowl. Spread onto crust. Layer with eggs and next 4 ingredients, in order. Sprinkle with basil and oregano. Bake in centre of 400°F (200°C) oven for 8 to 10 minutes until cheese is melted and crust is browned. Cuts into 8 wedges.

1 wedge: 230 Calories; 11 g Total Fat (2 g Mono, 0.5 g Poly, 5 g Sat); 185 mg Cholesterol; 19 g Carbohydrate; < 1 g Fibre; 14 g Protein; 460 mg Sodium

Peppered Egg Quesadilla

Quesadillas aren't just for dinner anymore! A nutritious and delicious hand-held breakfast that's sure to please the kids.

Whole-wheat flour tortillas (9 inch, 23 cm, diameter)	2	2
Grated jalapeño Monterey Jack cheese	2 tbsp.	30 mL
Canola oil	1/2 tsp.	2 mL
Sliced fresh white mushrooms	1/2 cup	125 mL
Chopped red pepper	1/4 cup	60 mL
Large eggs, fork-beaten	2	2
Chopped green onion	2 tbsp.	30 mL
Pepper	1/8 tsp.	0.5 mL
Grated jalapeño Monterey Jack cheese	2 tbsp.	30 mL

Preheat oven to 400°F (200°C). Place 1 tortilla on ungreased baking sheet. Sprinkle with first amount of cheese. Set aside.

Heat canola oil in medium non-stick frying pan on medium. Add mushrooms and red pepper. Cook for about 3 minutes, stirring occasionally, until red pepper is softened.

Add eggs. Sprinkle with green onion and pepper. Reduce heat to medium-low. Cook, covered, for about 2 minutes, without stirring, until eggs are set. Slide egg mixture onto tortilla on baking sheet.

Sprinkle with second amount of cheese. Place remaining tortilla on top. Bake in oven for about 3 minutes until cheese is melted. Cut into wedges. Serves 2.

1 serving: 274 Calories; 11.2 g Total Fat (4.2 g Mono, 1.6 g Poly, 4.5 g Sat); 199 mg Cholesterol; 37 g Carbohydrate; 4 g Fibre; 15 g Protein; 439 mg Sodium

Spiced Sweet Potato Hash

Start your morning off right with this colourful dish! Not only does it taste great, but the lowly sweet potato is a nutritional powerhouse. It is loaded with fibre and antioxidants, has anti-inflammatory properties and helps regulate blood sugar levels.

Cooking oil	1 tsp.	2 mL
Sausage, chopped	1 cup	250 mL
Cooking oil	2 tbsp.	30 mL
Cubed, peeled orange-fleshed sweet potato	3 cups	750 mL
Chopped green onion	1/2 cup	125 mL
Chopped red pepper	1/2 cup	125 mL
Chili powder	1/2 tsp.	2 mL
Paprika	1/2 tsp.	2 mL
Salt	1/2 tsp.	2 mL
Ground cinnamon	1/8 tsp.	0.5 mL

Heat first amount of cooking oil in medium frying pan on medium-high. Add sausage. Cook and stir for about 5 minutes, until sausage starts to brown. Remove from pan and set aside.

Heat second amount of cooking oil in pan on medium-high. Add sweet potato. Heat and stir for about 5 minutes until starting to brown. Reduce heat to medium-low.

Add remaining 6 ingredients. Stir. Cook, covered, for about 5 minutes, stirring occasionally, until sweet potato is tender. Makes about 4 cups (1 L).

1 cup: 290 Calories; 17 g Total Fat (4 g Mono, 2 g Poly, 4 g Sat); 25 mg Cholesterol; 25 g Carbohydrate; 4 g Fibre; 9 g Protein; 640 mg Sodium

Tofu Scramble

Tofu scramble is a staple for many vegetarians, but it is so tasty that non-vegetarians won't miss the meat. This dish is a great way to introduce tofu to those who may be a little hesitant to try it.

Package of firm tofu	14 oz.	396 g
Olive oil	2 tbsp.	30 mL
Red pepper, chopped	1/2 cup	125 mL
Mushrooms, sliced	1/2 cup	125 mL
Zucchini, chopped	1/2 cup	125 mL
Garlic clove, pressed	1	1
Dried oregano	1 tsp.	5 mL
Ground cumin	1 tsp.	5 mL
Salt	1/2 tsp.	2 mL
Pepper	1/2 tsp.	2 mL
Spinach, fresh	1 cup	250 mL
Tomato, chopped	1 cup	250 mL

Drain tofu and place it between two plates to squeeze out any excess water.

Heat oil in frying pan on medium. Add next 4 ingredients and cook, stirring constantly, for 5 minutes, until vegetables start to brown. Add tofu and cook, stirring, until it breaks up and starts to brown, about 3 minutes.

Add next 4 ingredients and cook, stirring, for 1 minute.

Add spinach and tomato. Cook until spinach wilts, about 2 minutes. Serves 2.

1 serving: 380 Calories; 26 g Total Fat (10 g Mono, 1.5 g Poly, 4.5 g Sat); 0 mg Cholesterol; 17 g Carbohydrate; 5 g Fibre; 25 g Protein; 620 mg Sodium

Ham and Asparagus Frittata

Because frittatas are easier to make, they are sometimes thought of as shortcuts for omelettes. Ham, asparagus and peppery eggs ensure there's no shortcut on flavour in this breakfast favourite.

Low-cholesterol egg product	2 cups	500 mL
Grated light sharp Cheddar cheese	1/4 cup	60 mL
Skim milk	1/4 cup	60 mL
Pepper	1/2 tsp.	2 mL
Tub margarine	4 tsp.	20 mL
Chopped fresh asparagus	2 cups	500 mL
Chopped no-fat deli ham	3/4 cup	175 mL
Chopped green onion	2 tbsp.	30 mL
Grated light sharp Cheddar cheese	1/4 cup	60 mL

Preheat broiler. Whisk first 4 ingredients in medium bowl.

Melt margarine in large non-stick frying pan on medium-high. Add next 3 ingredients. Stir-fry for about 3 minutes until asparagus is tender-crisp. Pour egg mixture over asparagus mixture. Reduce heat to medium-low. Cook, covered, for about 8 minutes until almost set. Remove from heat.

Sprinkle with second amount of cheese. Broil on centre rack (see Tip, below) for about 5 minutes until cheese is melted and eggs are set. Cuts into 6 wedges.

1 wedge: 138 Calories; 6.2 g Total Fat (1.1 g Mono, 1.0 g Poly, 1.6 g Sat); 79 mg Cholesterol; 5 g Carbohydrate; 1 g Fibre; 15 g Protein; 477 mg Sodium

Tip: When baking or broiling food in a frying pan with a handle that isn't ovenproof, wrap the handle in foil and keep it to the front of the oven, away from the element.

Big Breakfast Frittata

Start your busy day with a big breakfast frittata chock full of ham, mushrooms, peppers and cheese.

Cooking oil	1 tsp.	5 mL
Chopped deli ham	1 cup	250 mL
Sliced fresh white mushrooms	1 cup	250 mL
Chopped red pepper	1/2 cup	125 mL
Chopped green onion	1/4 cup	60 mL
Large eggs	8	8
Dried oregano	1/2 tsp.	2 mL
Salt, pinch		
Pepper, pinch		
Grated Cheddar cheese	1/2 cup	125 mL
Chopped tomato	1/2 cup	125 mL
Chopped green onion	1 tbsp.	15 mL

Heat cooking oil in large non-stick frying pan on medium. Add next 4 ingredients. Cook for about 5 minutes, stirring occasionally, until red pepper is softened.

Whisk next 4 ingredients in medium bowl. Pour over ham mixture. Reduce heat to medium-low. Cook, covered, for about 10 minutes until bottom is golden and top is set. Remove from heat.

Sprinkle with cheese. Let stand for about 1 minute until cheese is melted.

Sprinkle with tomato and second amount of green onion. Cuts into 4 wedges.

1 wedge: 253 Calories; 15.4 g Total Fat (2.0 g Mono, 0.5 g Poly, 6.1 g Sat); 461 mg Cholesterol; 6 g Carbohydrate; 1 g Fibre; 23 g Protein; 701 mg Sodium

Oven Omelette

Can't seem to get the hang of making omelettes in a frying pan? Try this oven method for quick and tasty results. All of the flavour with none of the fuss!

Low-cholesterol egg product	1 1/2 cups	375 mL
Finely chopped green onion	2 tbsp.	30 mL
Skim milk	2 tbsp.	30 mL
Salt	1/4 tsp.	1 mL
Pepper	1/8 tsp.	0.5 mL
Cooking spray		
Grated Swiss cheese	1/2 cup	125 mL
Deli turkey breast slices, cut into thin strips	2 oz.	57 g

Preheat oven to 400°F (200°C). Heat 9 x 13 inch (22 x 33 cm) baking dish in oven for 3 minutes. Meanwhile, combine first 5 ingredients in small bowl.

Spray hot baking dish with cooking spray. Pour egg mixture into dish. Bake, uncovered, for about 8 minutes until eggs start to set but are still moist on surface. Cut into 4 pieces. Sprinkle cheese and turkey onto half of each piece. Bake, uncovered, for about 2 minutes until cheese is melted. Fold omelettes over turkey and cheese. Makes 4 omelettes.

1 omelette: 132 Calories; 5.9 g Total Fat (0 g Mono, 0 g Poly, 2.5 g Sat); 95 mg Cholesterol; 3 g Carbohydrate; trace Fibre; 15 g Protein; 456 mg Sodium

Maple Turkey Egg Sandwiches

Maple-flavoured turkey patties and eggs nestled in whole-wheat English muffins—this sandwich will get your taste buds jumping!

Whole-wheat (or plain) English muffins, split	4	4
Butter	2 tbsp.	30 mL
Prepackaged egg white product	2 cups	500 mL
95% fat-free spreadable cream cheese	1 cup	250 mL
Skim milk	1/2 cup	125 mL
Raisin bread slice	1	1
Skim milk	2 tbsp.	30 mL
Grated peeled cooking apple (such as McIntosh)	1/4 cup	60 mL
Maple (or maple-flavoured) syrup	1 tbsp.	15 mL
Seasoned salt	1/2 tsp.	2 mL
Ground cinnamon	1/4 tsp.	1 mL
Poultry seasoning	1/4 tsp.	1 mL
Extra-lean ground turkey breast	1/2 lb.	225 g
Chopped fresh parsley, sprinkle		
Paprika, sprinkle		

Toast English muffin halves. Cover to keep warm.

Meanwhile, melt butter in large frying pan on medium.

Whisk next 3 ingredients in medium bowl until combined. Pour into frying pan. Cook and stir until set and liquid has evaporated.

Put bread slice into blender. Process until broken up into small pieces.

Preheat broiler. Combine next 6 ingredients and bread crumbs in medium bowl. Add turkey. Mix well. Divide into 4 equal portions. Shape into 2 1/2 inch (6.4 cm) diameter patties. Arrange on greased baking sheet with sides. Broil on top rack in oven for about 6 minutes per side until browned and internal temperature reaches 175°F (80°C).

Divide patties among bottom half of English muffins, spoon egg over patty, sprinkle with parsley and paprika, and top with remaining muffin halves. Serves 4.

1 serving: 460 Calories; 11 g Total Fat (2 g Mono, 0 g Poly, 6 g Sat); 65 mg Cholesterol; 44 g Carbohydrate; 4 g Fibre; 43 g Protein; 1140 mg Sodium

Double Strawberry Toast

Strawberries as far as the eye can see! These French toast sandwiches have strawberries inside and out. The honey, strawberry and lime topping adds that extra bit of delightful decadence.

Liquid honey	1/4 cup	60 mL
Lime juice	2 tbsp.	30 mL
Grated lime zest	1 tsp.	5 mL
Sliced fresh strawberries	3 cups	750 mL
Package of low-cholesterol egg product (see Note)	8 oz.	227 mL
Vanilla soy milk	1 cup	250 mL
Coconut (or vanilla) extract	1/2 tsp.	2 mL
Strawberry jam	2/3 cup	150 mL
Whole-grain bread slices	12	12
Canola oil	2 tbsp.	30 mL

Combine first 3 ingredients in medium bowl. Add strawberries. Stir well. Set aside.

Whisk next 3 ingredients in large shallow bowl until frothy. Set aside.

Spread about 1 1/2 tbsp. (25 mL) jam on 1 bread slice. Cover with second bread slice. Repeat with remaining jam and bread slices, making 6 sandwiches.

Heat 1 tbsp. (15 mL) canola oil in large frying pan on medium-low. Press one sandwich into egg mixture. Turn over to coat both sides. Transfer to frying pan. Repeat with 2 more sandwiches. Cook for about 4 minutes per side until golden. Transfer to serving platter. Keep warm in 200°F (95°C) oven. Repeat with remaining oil, sandwiches and egg mixture. Spoon 1/2 cup (125 mL) strawberry mixture over each sandwich. Makes 6 sandwiches.

1 sandwich: 399 Calories; 8.6 g Total Fat (4.0 g Mono, 2.1 g Poly, 1.2 g Sat); 32 mg Cholesterol; 71 g Carbohydrate; 6 g Fibre; 12 g Protein; 336 mg Sodium

Note: You can use 4 large, fork-beaten eggs instead of the low-cholesterol egg product, if you prefer.

Creamy Couscous Parfaits

This blend of fruit, yogurt and whole grains makes for a hearty breakfast and is also good as a healthy dessert.

Skim milk	2/3 cup	150 mL
Salt, pinch		
Whole-wheat couscous	1/3 cup	75 mL
Can of pineapple tidbits, drained and juice reserved	14 oz.	398 mL
Coarsely chopped kiwifruit	1 cup	250 mL
Coarsely chopped strawberries	1 cup	250 mL
Reserved pineapple juice	1/4 cup	60 mL
Chopped fresh mint	2 tbsp.	30 mL
Light sour cream	1/2 cup	125 mL
Non-fat peach yogurt	1/2 cup	125 mL
Liquid honey	1 tbsp.	15 mL
Minced crystallized ginger	1 tsp.	5 mL
Grated orange zest	1/2 tsp.	2 mL

Combine milk and salt in small saucepan. Bring to a boil. Add couscous. Stir. Remove from heat. Let stand, covered, for about 5 minutes until tender. Fluff with fork. Spread on baking sheet with sides. Freeze for 5 minutes.

Meanwhile, combine next 5 ingredients in medium bowl. Let stand for 15 minutes, stirring occasionally.

Combine remaining 5 ingredients in separate medium bowl. Add chilled couscous. Stir. Spoon half of fruit mixture into 4 parfait glasses or small bowls. Spoon couscous mixture over fruit. Top with remaining fruit mixture. Makes 4 parfaits.

1 parfait: 223 Calories; 3.1 g Total Fat (trace Mono, 0.1 Poly, 1.6 g Sat); 11 mg Cholesterol; 43 g Carbohydrate; 5 g Fibre; 6 g Protein; 67 mg Sodium

Maui Oatmeal

A healthy breakfast treat bursting with sweet tropical flavours.

Can of crushed pineapple (with juice)	14 oz.	398 mL
Chopped dried apricot	1/2 cup	125 mL
Medium sweetened coconut	1/2 cup	125 mL
Water	2 1/2 cups	625 mL
Salt, pinch		
Quick-cooking rolled oats	1 1/2 cups	375 mL

Combine first 3 ingredients in medium saucepan. Add water and salt. Heat on medium, stirring occasionally, until boiling.

Add rolled oats. Stir. Reduce heat to medium-low. Heat and stir for about 3 minutes until thickened. Remove from heat. Serve immediately or let stand until desired thickness. Serves 6.

1 serving: 460 Calories; 5.2 g Total Fat (0.9 g Mono, 0.8 g Poly, 2.9 g Sat); 0 mg Cholesterol; 104 g Carbohydrate; 13 g Fibre; 8 g Protein; 34 mg Sodium

Pumpkin-spice Oatmeal

Why wait until fall to have your favourite coffee flavours when you can have them year-round in a healthy breakfast. For a milder flavour, cut the spices in half. Sprinkle with roasted pumpkin seeds to add a little texture

Water	1 1/2 cup	375 mL
Apple juice	1/2 cup	125 mL
Quick-cooking rolled oats	1 1/4 cups	300 mL
Ground cinnamon	1 tsp.	5 mL
Ground nutmeg	1 tsp.	5 mL
Ground ginger	1/2 tsp.	2 mL
Ground cloves	1/4 tsp.	1 mL
Honey	3 tbsp.	45 mL
Pumpkin purée	1/4 cup	60 mL
Milk (optional)	1 cup	250 mL

Bring water and apple juice to a boil in medium saucepan.

Combine next 5 ingredients in small bowl and add to saucepan. Cook for 1 minute, stirring occasionally. Remove from heat and stir in honey and pumpkin purée.

Divide mixture among 4 bowls and add milk, if using. Serves 4.

1 serving: 170 Calories; 2.5 g Total Fat (1 g Mono, 1 g Poly, 0.5 g Sat); 0 mg Cholesterol; 34 g Carbohydrate; 4 g Fibre; 4 g Protein; 0 mg Sodium

Cinnamon Apple Grits

You may not want to kiss these grits, but you'll probably want to kiss the cook who made them! This sunny yellow cornmeal mixture with an apple, raisin and walnut topping provides sweet relief from everyday oatmeal.

Chopped, peeled cooking apple (such as McIntosh)	1 1/2 cups	375 mL
Frozen concentrated apple juice, thawed	1 cup	250 mL
Water	1/2 cup	125 mL
Golden raisins	1/2 cup	125 mL
Liquid honey	2 tbsp.	30 mL
Ground cinnamon	1 tsp.	5 mL
Water	3 1/2 cups	875 mL
Frozen concentrated apple juice, thawed	1/2 cup	125 mL
Salt	1/2 tsp.	2 mL
Yellow cornmeal	1 cup	250 mL
Coarsely chopped walnuts	1/2 cup	125 mL

Combine first 6 ingredients in medium saucepan. Bring to a boil. Reduce heat to medium. Boil gently, uncovered, for 10 minutes.

Meanwhile, combine next 3 ingredients in large saucepan. Bring to a boil. Slowly add cornmeal, stirring constantly. Reduce heat to low. Cook for 3 to 5 minutes, stirring often, until thickened to consistency of soft porridge.

Add walnuts to apple mixture. Stir. Spoon cornmeal mixture into 4 individual serving bowls. Spoon apple mixture over top. Serves 4.

1 serving: 517 Calories; 10.9 g Total Fat (1.5 g Mono, 7.5 g Poly, 1.1 g Sat); 0 mg Cholesterol; 103 g Carbohydrate; 5 g Fibre; 7 g Protein; 323 mg Sodium

Make-ahead Eggs Benedict

Make-ahead convenience without sacrificing any the dish's signature rich creaminess. Ideal for special occasions.

English muffins, split	4	4
Bacon slices	16	16
White vinegar	1 tsp.	5 mL
Large eggs	8	8
SAUCE		
Hard margarine (or butter)	1/4 cup	60 mL
All-purpose flour	1/4 cup	60 mL
Paprika	1 tsp.	5 mL
Pepper	1/4 tsp.	1 mL
Ground nutmeg	1/8 tsp.	0.5 mL
Milk	2 cups	500 mL
Grated Swiss cheese	2 cups	500 mL
Dry white (or alcohol-free) wine	1/2 cup	125 mL
TOPPING (optional)		
Hard margarine (or butter)	1 tbsp.	15 mL
Crushed cornflakes cereal	1/2 cup	125 mL

Arrange muffin halves, cut side up, in greased 9 x 13 inch (22 x 33 cm) pan.

Cook bacon in large frying pan on medium until crisp. Remove to paper towels to drain. Place 2 slices on each muffin half.

Pour water into large saucepan to depth of 2 to 4 inches (5 to 10 cm). Add vinegar. Stir. Bring to a boil on medium-high. Reduce heat to medium. Break eggs, 1 at a time, into shallow dish. Slip each egg into water. Cook for 2 to 3 minutes until egg whites are set and yolks are just set. Remove eggs using slotted spoon. Place 1 egg on top of bacon on each muffin half.

Sauce: Melt margarine in medium saucepan. Add flour, paprika, pepper and nutmeg. Stir well. Add milk, stirring constantly, until boiling and thickened.

Add cheese and wine. Stir until cheese is melted. Spoon sauce over eggs.

Topping: Melt margarine in small saucepan. Add cereal. Stir. Sprinkle over sauce. Cover. Chill overnight. Remove cover. Bake in 375°F (190°C) oven for 20 to 25 minutes until hot. Serves 8.

1 serving (without topping): 680 Calories; 53 g Total Fat (22 g Mono, 7 g Poly, 20 g Sat); 290 mg Cholesterol; 23 g Carbohydrate; <1 g Fibre; 25 g Protein; 1070 mg Sodium

Make-ahead French Toast

Cinnamon and a caramel coating make French bread a breakfast treat.

Hard margarine (or butter)	1/4 cup	60 mL
Brown sugar, packed	1/2 cup	125 mL
French bread loaf (about 15 oz., 425 g, ends trimmed off and loaf cut into 1 inch (2.5 cm) slices for a total of 12 slices	1	1
Large eggs	4	4
Milk	1 1/2 cups	375 mL
Ground cinnamon	1/2 tsp.	2 mL
Vanilla	1/2 tsp.	2 mL
Icing (confectioner's) sugar, sprinkle		

Melt margarine in small saucepan on medium. Add brown sugar. Stir until well combined. Pour into greased 9 x 13 inch (22 x 33 cm) pan. Spread evenly.

Place bread slices in tight single layer on top of brown sugar mixture.

Beat next 4 ingredients in medium bowl. Pour over bread. Cover. Chill for at least 3 hours or overnight. Remove cover. Bake in 400°F (200°C) oven for 20 to 25 minutes until edges are browned and knife inserted in centre comes out clean. Sprinkle with icing sugar. Serves 6.

1 serving: 418 Calories; 14.3 g Total Fat (7.6 g Mono, 1.8 g Poly, 3.6 g Sat); 146 mg Cholesterol; 59 g Carbohydrate; 2 g Fibre; 13 g Protein; 608 mg Sodium

Baked Monte Cristo

The Monte Cristo sandwich, a variation of the French Croque Monsieur, is traditionally fried, but our make-ahead version is baked, meaning it is both super convenient and healthier than the original! Substitute the ham for turkey, if you prefer.

Multigrain bread slices	12	12
Dijon mustard	1/4 cup	60 mL
Swiss cheese slices	6	6
Black forest ham slices	6	6
Large eggs, fork beaten	8	8
Salt	1/2 tsp	2 mL
Pepper	1/4 tsp	1 mL
Milk	3/4 cup	175 mL
Grated Swiss cheese	1/2 cup	125 mL

Spread each slice of bread with Dijon. Add slice of cheese and ham to each of 6 bread slices and top with remaining bread slices. Cut each sandwich in half to make 12 triangles. Fit triangles in 9 x 13 (23 x 33 cm) or 3 quart (3 L) greased baking dish.

In a medium bowl combine eggs, salt, pepper and milk. Pour over sandwiches. Cover dish and place in fridge for at least 6 hours or overnight.

To cook, preheat oven to 375°F (190°C). Sprinkle dish with grated Swiss cheese and bake for 25 minutes until edges are golden and cheese is melted. Serves 6.

1 serving: 400 Calories; 17 g Total Fat (4.5 g Mono, 1 g Poly, 7 g Sat); 315 mg Cholesterol; 42 g Carbohydrate; 6 g Fibre; 27 g Protein; 930 mg Sodium

Mexican Breakfast Bake

This attractive, tasty dish is a real time-saver in the morning because you do most of the work the night before. Add a little extra chipotle pepper if you want a spicy kick to get your morning started.

Olive oil	1 tsp.	5 mL
Medium onion, chopped	1	1
Garlic cloves, chopped	2	2
Can of chopped chilies	4 1/2 oz.	127 mL
Diced green pepper	1 cup	250 mL
Peeled and diced yam, cut into 1/4-inch, 6 mm, pieces	3 cups	750 mL
Medium tomatoes, cut into 1/4-inch, 6 mm, dice	2	2
Canned black beans, drained and rinsed (or cooked black beans)	2 cups	500 mL
Ground cumin	1 tsp.	5 mL
Ground chipotle pepper	1 tsp.	5 mL
Dried oregano	1/2 tsp.	2 mL
Paprika	1/2 tsp.	2 mL
Large eggs	4	4
Finely chopped cilantro leaves	1/4 cup	60 mL
Grated cheddar cheese	1/4 cup	60 mL
Diced avocado	1/4 cup	60 mL

Heat oil in large saucepot on medium-high. Add next 5 ingredients. Cook for 5 minutes.

Add next 6 ingredients. Cover and cook for 20 minutes until potatoes soften. Transfer to bowl, cover and refrigerate overnight.

To prepare dish, place 1 cup (250 mL) vegetable mixture in each of four 16 oz. (454 mL) ramekins sprayed with cooking spray. Microwave on high for 1 to 2 minutes. Make a well in centre of each and crack 1 egg in well. Bake in 450°F (230°C) oven for 5 minutes until whites are no longer translucent. Set oven to broil on High. Broil for 5 minutes until eggs are set. Remove from oven and sprinkle each dish with cilantro, cheese and avocado. Serve immediately. Serves 4.

1 serving: 490 Calories; 17 g Total Fat (8 g Mono, 2 g Poly, 4.5 g Sat); 220 mg Cholesterol; 60 g Carbohydrate; 16 g Fibre; 21 g Protein; 460 mg Sodium

Omelette Pork Rolls

Oriental-flavoured "egg rolls." These crêpe-like omelettes are wrapped around a delicious pork filling. Make the filling the night before, and prepare the omelettes in the morning. The omelettes can also be made ahead, if you are really pressed for time in the morning, but they taste best when fresh.

Cooking oil	2 tsp.	10 mL
Garlic cloves, minced	2	2
Finely chopped green onion	1/3 cup	75 mL
Sliced fresh white mushrooms	1 cup	250 mL
Lean ground pork	1 lb.	454 g
Finely chopped water chestnuts	1/3 cup	75 mL
Oyster sauce	3 tbsp.	45 mL
Sweet (or regular) chili sauce	2 tbsp.	30 mL
Dry sherry	1 tbsp.	15 mL
Soy sauce	2 tsp.	10 mL
Large eggs	6	6
Milk	2 tbsp.	30 mL
Hard margarine (or butter)	4 tsp.	20 mL

Heat cooking oil in large non-stick frying pan on medium. Add garlic, green onion and mushrooms. Cook for about 5 minutes, stirring often, until mushrooms are lightly browned.

Increase heat to medium-high. Add ground pork. Scramble-fry for 5 to 10 minutes until pork is lightly browned and no longer pink.

Add next 5 ingredients. Stir until well combined. Transfer to large bowl. Cover and refrigerate overnight.

Beat eggs and milk with whisk in medium bowl until smooth. Melt 1 tsp. (5 mL) margarine in same frying pan on medium. Pour 1/4 of egg mixture into frying pan, tilting pan to cover bottom. Cook for about 2 minutes until top is almost set and bottom is golden. Gently slide out of pan onto plate. Cover to keep warm. Repeat with remaining margarine and egg mixture to make 3 more omelettes. Lay 1 omelette on work surface. Place 1/4 of pork mixture along centre of omelette. Roll up, tucking in sides to enclose filling, being careful not to tear. Repeat with remaining omelettes and pork mixture. Makes 4 rolls.

1 roll: 381 Calories; 20.4 g Total Fat (9.7 g Mono, 2.8 g Poly, 5.6 g Sat); 391 mg Cholesterol; 12 g Carbohydrate; 1 g Fibre; 35 g Protein; 1451 mg Sodium

Buckwheat Sunrise

Watch out, oatmeal! Tangy orange and cranberries turn buckwheat into a serious contender for favourite breakfast grain. Make this the night before for a fast breakfast in the morning. For a little variety, try substituting chopped dried cherries for the cranberries.

Water	1 1/2 cups	375 mL
Whole buckwheat	1 cup	250 mL
Grated orange zest	1 tsp.	5 mL
Salt	1/4 tsp.	1 mL
Orange juice	1 cup	250 mL
Chopped dried apricot	1/3 cup	75 mL
Dried cranberries	1/3 cup	75 mL
Liquid honey	3 tbsp.	45 mL
Slivered almonds, toasted (see Tip, page 52)	1/4 cup	60 mL

Combine first 4 ingredients in medium saucepan. Bring to a boil. Reduce heat to medium-low. Simmer, covered, for about 15 minutes, without stirring, until buckwheat is tender.

Add orange juice. Stir. Add next 3 ingredients. Stir. Transfer to medium bowl. Cool at room temperature before covering. Chill for at least 6 hours or overnight until apricot and cranberries are softened and liquid is absorbed.

Add almonds. Stir. Makes about 3 cups (750 mL).

1 cup (250 mL): 367 Calories; 6.1 g Total Fat (3.3 g Mono, 1.6 g Poly, 0.7 g Sat); 0 mg Cholesterol; 76 g Carbohydrate; 6 g Fibre; 8 g Protein; 210 mg Sodium

Slow Cooker Steel Cut Oatmeal

Turn the slow cooker on just before you go to bed, and wake up to the delicious aroma of vanilla and maple. Once you take off the lid, the whole house will smell amazing! Tasty and nutritious, a serving of this oatmeal provides a big boost of complex carbohydrates and 10 percent of your daily requirement of iron to keep you going all morning long. Top with your favourite jam for a lovely presentation.

Steel cut oats	2 cups	500 mL
Water	7 cups	1.5 L
Salt	1/4 tsp	1 mL
Maple syrup	3 tbsp.	45 mL
Dark brown sugar	3 tbsp.	45 mL
Vanilla bean	1	1
Chopped walnuts, toasted (see Tip, page 52)	3 tbsp.	45 mL

Combine first 5 ingredients in a 3 1/2 quart (3.5 L) slow cooker. Cut vanilla bean in half and scrape seeds into oats. Cover and cook on Low for 7 to 8 hours or on High for 3 1/2 hours.

Before serving, stir in walnuts. Serves 6.

1 serving: 200 Calories; 4.5 g Total Fat (1 g Mono, 2.5 g Poly, 0.5 g Sat); 0 mg Cholesterol; 36 g Carbohydrate; 4 g Fibre; 5 g Protein; 75 mg Sodium

Fruited Muesli

Start the day off right with this blend of fruits, nuts and oats. It can be stored in an airtight container in the refrigerator for up to four days.

Apple juice	1/2 cup	125 mL
Water	1/2 cup	125 mL
Large flake rolled oats	1 cup	250 mL
Chopped unpeeled cooking apple (such as McIntosh)	2 cups	500 mL
Plain yogurt	2 cups	500 mL
Chopped dried apricot	1/2 cup	125 mL
Raisins	1/2 cup	125 mL
Ground flaxseed (see Tip, page 50)	1/4 cup	60 mL
Sliced natural almonds, toasted (see Tip, page 52)	1/4 cup	60 mL
Unsalted, roasted sunflower seeds	1/4 cup	60 mL
Maple (or maple-flavoured) syrup	3 tbsp.	45 mL
Grated orange zest	1 tsp.	5 mL
Ground cinnamon	1 tsp.	5 mL

Combine apple juice and water in medium saucepan. Bring to a boil. Remove from heat. Add oats. Stir. Transfer to medium bowl. Chill for 25 to 30 minutes until liquid is absorbed.

Add remaining 10 ingredients. Stir. Makes about 6 cups (1.5 L).

1 cup (250 mL): 325 Calories; 10.7 g Total Fat (2.9 g Mono, 2.8 g Poly, 2.4 g Sat); 11 mg Cholesterol; 52 g Carbohydrate; 7 g Fibre; 9 g Protein; 51 mg Sodium

Orange Granola

Crispy orange-and-cinnamon flavoured oats with toasted almonds, coconut and sweet apricots make the perfect breakfast cereal—whether over yogurt or drenched in milk. Keep extras in the fridge for up to two weeks.

Liquid honey	1/4 cup	60 mL
Frozen concentrated orange juice	2 tbsp.	30 mL
Vanilla extract	1 tbsp.	15 mL
Canola oil	2 tsp.	10 mL
Ground cinnamon	1 tsp.	5 mL
Grated orange zest (optional)	1 tsp.	5 mL
Large flake rolled oats	3 cups	750 mL
Finely chopped dried apricot	1/2 cup	125 mL
Medium sweetened coconut	1/4 cup	60 mL
Sliced natural almonds	1/4 cup	60 mL

Preheat oven to 375°F (190°C). Combine first 6 ingredients in small dish. Reserve 2 tbsp. (30 mL) in small cup. Set aside.

Put oats into medium bowl. Drizzle honey mixture over top. Stir until coated. Spread evenly on greased baking sheet with sides. Bake for about 5 minutes, stirring occasionally, until starting to crisp and lightly brown.

Meanwhile, combine remaining 3 ingredients in small bowl. Drizzle reserved honey mixture over top. Stir until coated. Add to oat mixture. Stir. Bake for 4 to 6 minutes until crisp and golden. Transfer baking sheet to wire rack to cool. Makes about 4 cups (1 L). Serves 8.

1 serving: 232 Calories; 5.8 g Total Fat (2.0 g Mono, 0.8 g Poly, 0.9 g Sat); 0 mg Cholesterol; 38 g Carbohydrate; 4 g Fibre; 7 g Protein; 12 mg Sodium

Baked Breakfast Pears

This elegant dish is deceptively easy to prepare and is a welcome break from standard breakfast fare. Pears are available year-round but are in season from June to February, and there are many varieties to choose from. Bosc pears are one of the most popular for baking and poaching because they keep their shape when cooked.

Large, ripe, firm pears	4	4
Lemon juice	1 tbsp.	15 mL
Cinnamon sticks, broken in half	2	2
Agave syrup	2 tbsp.	30 mL
Apple juice	1/3 cup	75 mL
Vanilla bean	1/2	1/2
Vanilla Greek yogurt	1 cup	250 mL
Chopped pear	2 tbsp	30 mL
Chopped walnuts, toasted	2 tbsp.	30 mL
(see Tip, page 52)		
Cooking spray		

Preheat oven to 350°F (175°C). Spray 9 x 13 inch (23 x 33 cm) baking dish with cooking spray. Halve pears and core, removing a 1 inch (2.5 cm) deep scoop. Brush halves with lemon juice.

Combine next 3 ingredients in small bowl. Cut vanilla bean in half and scrape seeds into baking dish. Arrange pears, cut side up, in single layer in dish. Bake for 40 to 45 minutes, basting pears with apple juice mixture a few times, until pears are tender. Remove from oven and allow to cool completely. Cover and chill for at least 6 hours or overnight, turning pears in liquid at least twice during chilling time.

To serve, combine yogurt and apples. Spoon mixture into pear halves and sprinkle with walnuts. Serves 8.

1 serving: 130 Calories; 4 g Total Fat (0 g Mono, 1 g Poly, 2 g Sat); 5 mg Cholesterol; 24 g Carbohydrate; 3 g Fibre; 2 g Protein; 20 mg Sodium

Breakfast Kebabs

Beat the morning blahs with these creative kebabs! Fun to eat and oh so tasty!

Baby potatoes, unpeeled, cut in half	3	3
Bacon slices	6	6
Red pepper, cut in 1 inch (2.5 cm) pieces	1/2	1/2
Green pepper, cut in 1 inch (2.5 cm) pieces	1/2	1/2
Yellow pepper, cut in 1 inch (2.5 cm) pieces	1/2	1/2
Mushrooms	6	6
Cherry tomatoes	6	6
Pineapple cubes (1 inch, 2.5 cm pieces)	6	6
Strawberries, end trimmed	6	6
Ketchup	1/4 cup	60 mL
Balsamic vinegar	2 tbsp.	30 mL
Soy sauce	1 tbsp.	15 mL
Dijon mustard	1 tbsp.	15 mL
Honey	1 tbsp.	15 mL
Worcestershire sauce	1 tsp.	5 mL
Cayenne pepper	1/2 tsp.	2 mL
Lemon juice	1 tsp.	5 mL

Fill medium saucepan with enough water to cover potatoes. Cook over medium until almost tender, about 10 minutes. Drain and set aside until cool.

Preheat grill. Arrange ingredients on skewers in the following order: potato half, cherry tomato, pineapple, bacon, red pepper, green pepper, yellow pepper, mushroom and strawberry.

For sauce, combine remaining 8 ingredients in small bowl. Brush skewers with sauce. Transfer skewers to grill and cook until heated through, turning and brushing with sauce several times. Makes 6 skewers.

1 skewer: 180 Calories; 12 g Total Fat (5 g Mono, 1.5 g Poly, 4 g Sat); 13 mg Cholesterol; 14 g Carbohydrate; 1 g Fibre; 5 g Protein; 540 mg Sodium

Creamy Eggs on Mushrooms

Portobello mushrooms stuffed with a savoury egg filling make a hearty and delicious breakfast.

Olive (or canola) oil	2 tbsp.	30 mL
Garlic clove, minced	1	1
Large whole portobello mushrooms (about 5 inch, 12.5 cm, diameter)	4	4
Olive (or canola) oil	1 tbsp.	15 mL
Chopped onion	1/2 cup	125 mL
Diced red pepper	1/2 cup	125 mL
Garlic clove, minced	1	1
All-purpose flour	4 tsp.	20 mL
Low-sodium prepared chicken broth	2/3 cup	150 mL
Whipping cream	1/4 cup	60 mL
Large hard-cooked eggs, chopped	4	4
Seasoned salt	1/2 tsp.	2 mL
Dill weed	1/4 tsp.	1 mL
Pepper	1/8 tsp.	0.5 mL
Finely chopped fresh parsley	1 tbsp.	15 mL

Combine olive oil and garlic in small cup. Remove mushroom stems with knife. Remove and discard dark gills with spoon. Brush olive oil mixture on both sides of each mushroom. Preheat electric grill for 5 minutes or gas barbecue to medium (see Note). Cook mushrooms on greased grill for about 5 minutes per side until grill marks appear and mushrooms are tender. Transfer to large plate. Cover to keep warm.

Heat second amount of olive oil in large frying pan on medium. Add onion. Cook for 5 to 10 minutes, stirring often, until softened.

Add red pepper and second amount of garlic. Cook for 2 to 3 minutes, stirring often, until red pepper is tender-crisp.

Add flour. Heat and stir for 1 minute.

Slowly add broth and whipping cream, stirring constantly. Heat and stir for about 5 minutes until boiling and thickened.

(continued on next page)

Add next 4 ingredients. Stir until heated through. Makes 2 cups (500 mL) filling. Divide and spoon into mushroom caps.

Sprinkle each with parsley. Makes 4 stuffed mushrooms. Serves 4.

1 serving: *279 Calories; 21.4 g Total Fat (11.1 g Mono, 2 g Poly, 6.3 g Sat); 234 mg Cholesterol; 13 g Carbohydrate; 3 g Fibre; 11 g Protein; 330 mg Sodium*

Note: Mushrooms may be broiled in the oven. Place them on a greased broiler pan. Broil about 4 inches (10 cm) from the heat for about 5 minutes per side until tender.

Salmon Feta Frittata

*Wow your nearest and dearest with this delicious salmon, onion and egg dish—
complemented with Dijon mustard and feta cheese.*

Canola oil	1 tbsp.	15 mL
Large eggs	6	6
Milk	1 1/3 cups	325 mL
Dijon mustard	1 tbsp.	15 mL
Lemon pepper	1/4 tsp.	1 mL
Can of pink salmon, drained, skin and round bones removed	6 1/2 oz.	184 g
Crumbled light feta cheese	1/4 cup	60 mL
Chopped green onion	2 tbsp.	30 mL

Preheat broiler. Heat canola oil in large frying pan on medium.

Meanwhile, whisk next 4 ingredients in medium bowl until combined. Pour
into frying pan. Cook, uncovered, without stirring, for 5 minutes.

Sprinkle with remaining 3 ingredients. Cook, covered, for about 5 minutes
until bottom is golden and top is almost set. Remove from heat. Broil
on centre rack in oven for about 2 minutes until golden and set (see Tip,
page 96). Serves 4.

*1 serving: 244 Calories; 14.2 g Total Fat (5.4 g Mono, 2.2 g Poly, 3.7 g Sat); 316 mg Cholesterol;
5 g Carbohydrate; trace Fibre; 24 g Protein; 471 mg Sodium*

Weekend Brunch Dish

Loaded with bacon, green pepper and two kinds of cheese, this casserole's definitely a one-stop brunch dish!

Bacon slices, diced	6	6
Chopped green pepper	1/4 cup	60 mL
Chopped onion	1/4 cup	60 mL
Frozen hash brown potatoes, thawed	2 cups	500 mL
Large eggs	4	4
Water	1/4 cup	60 mL
Salt	1/2 tsp.	2 mL
Pepper	1/8 tsp.	0.5 mL
Grated medium Cheddar cheese	1/2 cup	125 mL
Grated part-skim mozzarella cheese	1/2 cup	125 mL
Chopped fresh parsley, for garnish		

Combine first 3 ingredients in large non-stick frying pan on medium. Cook for 5 to 10 minutes, stirring often, until bacon is crisp. Remove with slotted spoon to paper towel to drain. Drain all but 1 tbsp. (15 mL) drippings from pan.

Press hash browns evenly in same frying pan. Cook, uncovered, for about 10 minutes on medium-low, stirring occasionally, until crisp.

Beat next 4 ingredients in small bowl. Add bacon mixture. Stir. Pour over hash browns.

Sprinkle with half of Cheddar and mozzarella. Cook for about 5 minutes, stirring occasionally, until almost set. Turn oven to broil with rack in middle. Remove casserole from pan and place in 8 x 8 inch (20 x 20 cm) baking dish. Sprinkle with remaining cheese and broil for 5 minutes. Garnish with parsley. Serves 4.

1 serving: 289 Calories; 19.5 g Total Fat (7.4 g Mono, 1.8 g Poly, 8.8 g Sat); 224 mg Cholesterol; 10 g Carbohydrate; 1 g Fibre; 19 g Protein; 750 mg Sodium

Apple Raisin French Toast

With a sweet apple cinnamon topping, this raisin French toast is simply magnifique!

APPLE CINNAMON TOPPING

Chopped peeled cooking apple (such as McIntosh)	1 cup	250 mL
Apple juice	2 tbsp.	30 mL
Brown sugar, packed	1 tbsp.	15 mL
Ground cinnamon	1/8 tsp.	0.5 mL

RAISIN FRENCH TOAST

Large egg	1	1
Egg whites (large)	2	2
Skim milk	1/4 cup	60 mL
Raisin bread slices	4	4
Cooking spray		

Apple Cinnamon Topping: Combine all 4 ingredients in small saucepan. Cover. Bring to a boil. Reduce heat to medium. Cook, uncovered, for about 5 minutes, stirring occasionally, until apple is tender. Makes about 1/2 cup (125 mL) topping.

Raisin French Toast: Meanwhile, whisk first 3 ingredients in small, shallow bowl.

Dip 1 bread slice in egg mixture. Turn to coat both sides. Place on large plate. Repeat with remaining bread slices. Pour remaining egg mixture over top. Heat large frying pan on medium. Spray with cooking spray. Arrange bread slices in single layer in frying pan. Cook for about 2 minutes per side until browned. Transfer bread slices to 2 serving plates. Spoon Apple Cinnamon Topping over top. Serves 2.

1 serving: 271 Calories; 4.9 g Total Fat (2.3 g Mono, 0.8 g Poly, 1.4 g Sat); 94 mg Cholesterol; 46 g Carbohydrate; 4 g Fibre; 12 g Protein; 307 mg Sodium

Banana Maple French Toast

Who doesn't have time for a quick, sweet treat? Try this golden French toast with maple-fried bananas next time you're craving a sweet breakfast.

FRENCH TOAST

Butter	1 tbsp.	15 mL
Large eggs	2	2
Milk	1/2 cup	125 mL
Granulated sugar	2 tsp.	10 mL
Salt, sprinkle		
White (or whole-wheat) bread slices	4	4

BANANA TOPPING

Butter	1 tbsp.	15 mL
Sliced banana (1/2 inch, 12 mm, slices)	2 cups	500 mL
Maple syrup	1/4 cup	60 mL

French Toast: Melt butter in large frying pan on medium.

Meanwhile, whisk next 4 ingredients in small shallow bowl.

Dip bread slices into egg mixture. Turn to coat both sides. Add to pan. Pour any remaining egg mixture over top. Cook for about 2 minutes per side until browned. Transfer to 4 serving plates.

Banana Topping: Melt butter in medium frying pan on medium. Add banana. Heat and stir for 1 minute.

Add syrup. Stir. Spoon banana topping over toast. Serves 4.

1 serving: 292 Calories; 9.4 g Total Fat (1.8 g Mono, 0.6 g Poly, 4.8 g Sat); 124 mg Cholesterol; 47 g Carbohydrate; 3 g Fibre; 7 g Protein; 262 mg Sodium

Dutch Baby with Spiced Fruit

Dutch babies were introduced in the early 1900s in a cafe in Seattle, Washington. They were based on German pancakes and were originally served as three small "babies" topped with icing sugar and a squeeze of lemon juice. Over time, the "Big Dutch baby" emerged, often served with fruit in the middle, and it is this variation that is most often seen in restaurants today.

All-purpose flour	1/2 cup	125 mL
Salt	1/2 tsp.	2 mL
Large eggs	2	2
Milk	1/2 cup	125 mL
Butter, melted	2 tbsp.	30 mL
Butter, melted	2 tbsp.	30 mL
Peach slices, fresh or frozen	1 1/2 cups	375 mL
Strawberries, quartered	1 1/4 cups	300 mL
Ground cinnamon	1/2 tsp.	2 mL
Ground ginger	1/2 tsp.	2 mL
Agave syrup	2 tbsp.	30 mL
Lemon juice	1 tbsp.	15 mL
Icing (confectioner's) sugar	2 tsp.	10 mL
Yogurt	1/4 cup	60 mL
Lemon zest	1 tsp.	5 mL

Combine flour and salt in small bowl.

Blend eggs in blender on low speed. Add flour mixture and milk alternately in 6 additions. Blend until smooth. Add butter. Blend. Pour mixture into a greased ovenproof skillet. Bake in 450°F (230°C) oven for 20 minutes. Reduce heat to 350°F (175°C) and bake for an additional 10 minutes.

For the spiced fruit, heat remaining butter in medium frying pan on high. Add next 5 ingredients and cook until peaches begin to brown, about 6 minutes.

Remove skillet from oven. Drizzle Dutch baby with lemon juice and spread fruit mixture over top. Sprinkle with icing sugar and top with yogurt and lemon zest. Makes 6 to 8 servings.

1 serving: 190 Calories; 10 g Total Fat (2.5 g Mono, 0.5 g Poly, 6 g Sat); 90 mg Cholesterol; 23 g Carbohydrate; 2 g Fibre; 5 g Protein; 290 mg Sodium

Wild Rice Apricot Pancakes

These deliciously addictive, fluffy pancakes include chewy wild rice and apricot for an interesting texture contrast. So flavourful, you could easily skip out on the butter and syrup!

Large eggs, fork-beaten	2	2
Cooked wild rice	1/2 cup	125 mL
Chopped dried apricot	1/3 cup	75 mL
Skim milk	1/3 cup	75 mL
Unsweetened applesauce	2 tbsp.	30 mL
Buttermilk pancake mix	2/3 cup	150 mL
Canola oil	2 tsp.	10 mL

Combine first 5 ingredients in small bowl. Add pancake mix. Stir until just moistened. Batter will be lumpy.

Heat 1/2 tsp. (2 mL) canola oil in large frying pan on medium. Pour batter into pan, using 1/2 cup (125 mL) for each pancake. Cook for about 2 minutes until bubbles form on top and edges appear dry. Turn pancake over. Cook for about 2 minutes until golden. Remove to plate. Cover to keep warm. Repeat with remaining batter, heating more canola oil if necessary to prevent sticking. Makes about 4 pancakes. Serves 2.

1 pancake: 198 Calories; 5.4 g Total Fat (2.7 g Mono, 1.2 g Poly, 1.0 g Sat); 93 mg Cholesterol; 31 g Carbohydrate; 2 g Fibre; 8 g Protein; 434 mg Sodium

Buckwheat Peach Pancakes

Good morning, sunshine! Make sure your day is warm and bright right from the start with these golden pancakes with sweet bits of peach. Great with peach jam or syrup.

All-purpose flour	1 1/4 cups	300 mL
Buckwheat flour	3/4 cup	175 mL
Granulated sugar	1/4 cup	60 mL
Baking soda	2 tsp.	10 mL
Ground cardamom	1/4 tsp.	1 mL
Salt	1/4 tsp.	1 mL
Large eggs, fork-beaten	3	3
Can of apricot halves in light syrup, drained and syrup reserved, chopped	14 oz.	398 mL
Milk	1 cup	250 mL
Reserved peach syrup	1/4 cup	60 mL
Canola oil	2 tbsp.	30 mL

Combine first 6 ingredients in large bowl. Make a well in centre.

Combine remaining 5 ingredients in medium bowl. Add to well. Stir until just moistened. Batter will be lumpy. Preheat griddle to medium-high (see Note). Reduce heat to medium. Spray with cooking spray. Pour batter onto griddle, using about 1/3 cup (75 mL) for each pancake. Cook for about 2 minutes until bubbles form on top and edges appear dry. Turn pancake over. Cook for about 2 minutes until golden. Remove to plate. Cover to keep warm. Repeat with remaining batter, spraying griddle with cooking spray if necessary to prevent sticking. Makes about 12 pancakes.

1 pancake: 156 Calories; 4.1 g Total Fat (2.0 g Mono, 1.0 g Poly, 0.8 g Sat); 47 mg Cholesterol; 26 g Carbohydrate; 1 g Fibre; 5 g Protein; 288 mg Sodium (is there a new one?)

Note: If you don't have an electric griddle, use a large frying pan. Heat 1 tsp. (5 mL) canola oil on medium. Heat more canola oil with each batch if necessary to prevent sticking.

Pumpkin Oatmeal Pancakes

Perfect comfort food for a chilly fall or winter morning. These pancakes are supremely kid-friendly.

All-purpose flour	1 cup	250 mL
Old-fashioned rolled oats	1 cup	250 mL
Brown sugar	3 tbsp.	45 mL
Baking powder	2 tsp.	10 mL
Baking soda	1 tsp.	5 mL
Ground cinnamon	1 tsp.	5 mL
Ground ginger	1/2 tsp.	2 mL
Ground cloves, sprinkle		
Salt	1/2 tsp.	2 mL
Milk	1 1/2 cups	375 mL
Pumpkin purée	1 cup	250 mL
Large egg	1	1
Cooking oil	2 tbsp.	30 mL
Vinegar	2 tbsp.	30 mL

In large bowl combine flour, oats, brown sugar, baking powder, baking soda, cinnamon, ginger, cloves and salt. Make a well in centre.

In separate bowl, mix together milk, pumpkin, egg, oil and vinegar. Add to well and stir just enough to combine. Heat a lightly oiled griddle or frying pan over medium-high. Pour batter onto griddle, using approximately 1/4 cup for each pancake. Cook until brown on both sides. Makes about 12 pancakes.

1 pancake: 130 Calories; 3.5 g Total Fat (1.5 g Mono, 1 g Poly, 0.5 g Sat); 20 mg Cholesterol; 20 g Carbohydrate; 2 g Fibre; 4 g Protein; 280 mg Sodium

Oven Apple Pancake

Eggy and sweet, this pancake has a pie-like quality that the whole family will love. It tastes great served with maple syrup and a side of sausages.

Butter or hard margarine	1/4 cup	60 mL
Brown sugar, packed	1/3 cup	75 mL
Ground cinnamon, light sprinkle		
Apples, peeled, cored and sliced in wedges 1/4 inch (6 mm) thick	2	2
Large eggs	3	3
Milk	3/4 cup	175 mL
Salt	1/2 tsp.	2 mL
All-purpose flour	3/4 cup	175 mL

Melt butter in 9 inch (23 cm) pie plate in 425°F (220°C) oven.

Stir brown sugar into melted butter. Sprinkle with cinnamon. Overlap apples in single layer. Cook in oven for 10 minutes.

Beat eggs in medium bowl. Add milk, salt and flour. Stir to moisten. Don't try to smooth out small lumps. Pour over apples. Return to oven. Bake for 20 to 25 minutes. Cut into wedges. Serves 6.

1 serving: 260 Calories; 11 g Total Fat (3 g Mono, 0.5 g Poly, 6 g Sat); 125 mg Cholesterol; 36 g Carbohydrate; 2 g Fibre; 6 g Protein; 310 mg Sodium

Baked Blueberry Pecan Oatmeal

A warm, comforting breakfast casserole. Blueberries add sweetness while pecans add delectable crunch. Top with yogurt for a real treat.

Quick-cooking rolled oats	2 cups	500 mL
Milk	1 1/4 cups	300 mL
Unsweetened applesauce	3/4 cup	175 mL
Dried blueberries (or cranberries)	1/2 cup	125 mL
Brown sugar, packed	1/4 cup	60 mL
Chopped pecans, toasted (see Tip, page 52)	1/4 cup	60 mL
Wheat germ	1/4 cup	60 mL
Butter (or hard margarine), melted	2 tbsp.	30 mL
Ground cinnamon	1 tsp.	5 mL
Vanilla extract	1 tsp.	5 mL
Ground ginger	1/2 tsp.	2 mL
Salt	1/2 tsp.	2 mL

Combine all 12 ingredients in medium bowl. Spread evenly in greased 8 x 8 inch (20 x 20 cm) baking dish. Bake, covered, in 350°F (175°C) oven for about 20 minutes until liquid is absorbed. Serves 4.

1 serving: 460 Calories; 15.0 g Total Fat (5.0 g Mono, 2.5 g Poly, 5.0 g Sat); 18 mg Cholesterol; 72 g Carbohydrate; 10 g Fibre; 12 g Protein; 336 mg Sodium

MEASUREMENT TABLES

Throughout this book measurements are given in Conventional and Metric measure. To compensate for differences between the two measurements due to rounding, a full metric measure is not always used. The cup used is the standard 8 fluid ounce. Temperature is given in degrees Fahrenheit and Celsius. Baking pan measurements are in inches and centimetres as well as quarts and litres. An exact metric conversion is given below as well as the working equivalent (Metric Standard Measure).

SPOONS

Conventional Measure	Metric Exact Conversion Millilitre (mL)	Metric Standard Measure Millilitre (mL)
1/8 teaspoon (tsp.)	0.6 mL	0.5 mL
1/4 teaspoon (tsp.)	1.2 mL	1 mL
1/2 teaspoon (tsp.)	2.4 mL	2 mL
1 teaspoon (tsp.)	4.7 mL	5 mL
2 teaspoons (tsp.)	9.4 mL	10 mL
1 tablespoon (tbsp.)	14.2 mL	15 mL

CUPS

Conventional Measure	Metric Exact Conversion Millilitre (mL)	Metric Standard Measure Millilitre (mL)
1/4 cup (4 tbsp.)	56.8 mL	60 mL
1/3 cup (5 1/3 tbsp.)	75.6 mL	75 mL
1/2 cup (8 tbsp.)	113.7 mL	125 mL
2/3 cup (10 2/3 tbsp.)	151.2 mL	150 mL
3/4 cup (12 tbsp.)	170.5 mL	175 mL
1 cup (16 tbsp.)	227.3 mL	250 mL
4 1/2 cups	1022.9 mL	1000 mL

DRY MEASURES

Conventional Measure	Metric Exact Conversion Grams (mL)	Metric Standard Measure Grams (mL)
1 oz.	28.3 g	28 g
2 oz.	56.7 g	57 g
3 oz.	85.0 g	85 g
4 oz.	113.4 g	125 g
5 oz.	141.7 g	140 g
6 oz.	170.1 g	170 g
7 oz.	198.4 g	200 g
8 oz.	226.8 g	250 g
16 oz.	453.6 g	500 g
32 oz.	907.2 g	1000 g

OVEN TEMPERATURES

Fahrenheit (°F)	Celsius (°C)
175°	80°
200°	95°
225°	110°
250°	120°
275°	140°
300°	150°
325°	160°
350°	175°
375°	190°
400°	205°
425°	220°
450°	230°
475°	240°
500°	260°

PANS

Conventional Inches	Metric Inches
8 x 8 inch	20 x 20 cm
9 x 9 inch	23 x 23 cm
9 x 13 inch	23 x 33 cm
10 x 15 inch	25 x 38 cm
11 x 17 inch	28 x 43 cm
8 x 2 inch round	20 x 5 cm
9 x 2 inch round	23 x 5 cm
10 x 4 1/2 inch tube	25 x 11 cm
8 x 4 x 3 inch loaf	20 x 10 x 7.5 cm
9 x 5 x 3 inch loaf	23 x 12.5 x 7.5 cm

CASSEROLES

CANADA & BRITAIN		UNITED STATES	
Standard Size Casserole	Exact Metric Measure	Standard Size Casserole	Exact Metric Measure
1 qt. (5 cups)	1.13 L	1 qt. (4 cups)	900 mL
1 1/2 qts. (7 1/2 cups)	1.69 L	1 1/2 qts. (6 cups)	1.35 L
2 qts. (10 cups)	2.25 L	2 qts. (8 cups)	1.8 L
2 1/2 qts. (12 1/2 cups)	2.81 L	2 1/2 qts. (10 cups)	2.25 L
3 qts. (15 cups)	3.38 L	3 qts. (12 cups)	2.7 L
4 qts. (20 cups)	4.5 L	4 qts. (16 cups)	3.6 L
5 qts. (25 cups)	5.63 L	5 qts. (20 cups)	4.5 L

INDEX